# USING GRAVESTONES TO TRACE YOUR ANCESTORS

# FAMILY HISTORY FROM PEN & SWORD BOOKS

*Birth, Marriage & Death Records*
*The Family History Web Directory*
*Tracing British Battalions on the Somme*
*Tracing Great War Ancestors*
*Tracing History Through Title Deeds*
*Tracing Secret Service Ancestors*
*Tracing the Rifle Volunteers*
*Tracing Your Air Force Ancestors*
*Tracing Your Ancestors*
*Tracing Your Ancestors from 1066 to 1837*
*Tracing Your Ancestors Through Death Records – Second Edition*
*Tracing Your Ancestors Through Family Photographs*
*Tracing Your Ancestors Through Letters and Personal Writings*
*Tracing Your Ancestors Using DNA*
*Tracing Your Ancestors Using the Census*
*Tracing your Ancestors Using the UK Timeline*
*Tracing Your Ancestors: Cambridgeshire, Essex, Norfolk and Suffolk*
*Tracing Your Aristocratic Ancestors*
*Tracing Your Army Ancestors*
*Tracing Your Army Ancestors – Third Edition*
*Tracing Your Birmingham Ancestors*
*Tracing Your Black Country Ancestors*
*Tracing Your Boer War Ancestors*
*Tracing Your British Indian Ancestors*
*Tracing Your Canal Ancestors*
*Tracing Your Channel Islands Ancestors*
*Tracing Your Church of England Ancestors*
*Tracing Your Criminal Ancestors*
*Tracing Your Docker Ancestors*
*Tracing Your East Anglian Ancestors*
*Tracing Your East End Ancestors*
*Tracing Your Family History on the Internet*
*Tracing Your Female Ancestors*
*Tracing Your First World War Ancestors*
*Tracing Your Freemason, Friendly Society and Trade Union Ancestors*
*Tracing Your Georgian Ancestors, 1714–1837*
*Tracing Your Glasgow Ancestors*
*Tracing Your Great War Ancestors: The Gallipoli Campaign*
*Tracing Your Great War Ancestors: The Somme*
*Tracing Your Great War Ancestors: Ypres*
*Tracing Your Huguenot Ancestors*
*Tracing Your Insolvent Ancestors*
*Tracing Your Irish Family History on the Internet*
*Tracing Your Jewish Ancestors*
*Tracing Your Jewish Ancestors – Second Edition*
*Tracing Your Labour Movement Ancestors*
*Tracing Your Legal Ancestors*
*Tracing Your Liverpool Ancestors*
*Tracing Your Liverpool Ancestors – Second Edition*
*Tracing Your London Ancestors*
*Tracing Your Medical Ancestors*
*Tracing Your Merchant Navy Ancestors*
*Tracing Your Northern Ancestors*
*Tracing Your Northern Irish Ancestors*
*Tracing Your Northern Irish Ancestors – Second Edition*
*Tracing Your Oxfordshire Ancestors*
*Tracing Your Pauper Ancestors*
*Tracing Your Police Ancestors*
*Tracing Your Potteries Ancestors*
*Tracing Your Pre-Victorian Ancestors*
*Tracing Your Prisoner of War Ancestors: The First World War*
*Tracing Your Railway Ancestors*
*Tracing Your Roman Catholic Ancestors*
*Tracing Your Royal Marine Ancestors*
*Tracing Your Rural Ancestors*
*Tracing Your Scottish Ancestors*
*Tracing Your Second World War Ancestors*
*Tracing Your Servant Ancestors*
*Tracing Your Service Women Ancestors*
*Tracing Your Shipbuilding Ancestors*
*Tracing Your Tank Ancestors*
*Tracing Your Textile Ancestors*
*Tracing Your Twentieth-Century Ancestors*
*Tracing Your Welsh Ancestors*
*Tracing Your West Country Ancestors*
*Tracing Your Yorkshire Ancestors*
*Writing Your Family History*
*Your Irish Ancestors*

# Using Gravestones to Trace Your Ancestors

*A Guide for Family Historians*

## AMANDA LEEDHAM

Pen & Sword
**FAMILY HISTORY**

First published in Great Britain in 2025 by
**PEN AND SWORD FAMILY HISTORY**
An imprint of
Pen & Sword Books Ltd
Yorkshire – Philadelphia

Copyright © Amanda Leedham 2025

ISBN 978 1 03611 061 1

The right of Amanda Leedham to be identified as Author of this work has been asserted by her in accordance with the Copyright, Designs and Patents Act 1988.

A CIP catalogue record for this book is available from the British Library.

All rights reserved. No part of this book may be reproduced, transmitted, downloaded, decompiled or reverse engineered in any form or by any means, electronic or mechanical including photocopying, recording or by any information storage and retrieval system, without permission from the Publisher in writing. No part of this book may be used or reproduced in any manner for the purpose of training artificial intelligence technologies or systems.

Typeset by Mac Style
Printed in the UK by CPI Group (UK) Ltd, Croydon, CR0 4YY.

The Publisher's authorised representative in the EU for product safety is Authorised Rep Compliance Ltd., Ground Floor, 71 Lower Baggot Street, Dublin D02 P593, Ireland.
www.arccompliance.com

For a complete list of Pen & Sword titles please contact

PEN & SWORD BOOKS LIMITED
47 Church Street, Barnsley, South Yorkshire, S70 2AS, England
E-mail: enquiries@pen-and-sword.co.uk
Website: www.pen-and-sword.co.uk
or
PEN AND SWORD BOOKS
1950 Lawrence Road, Havertown, PA 19083, USA
E-mail: uspen-and-sword@casematepublishers.com
Website: www.penandswordbooks.com

# CONTENTS

*Preface* — vi
*Picture Credits* — viii
*Acknowledgements* — ix
*List of Abbreviations* — x
*Introduction* — xi
*Practicalities of Researching Gravestones* — xiv

**Chapter 1**  Symbolism, Wording and Beliefs — 1

**Chapter 2**  Children, Family and Ancestors — 19

**Chapter 3**  Occupations — 36

**Chapter 4**  Military Gravestones and Commemorations — 54

**Chapter 5**  How People Died — 78

**Chapter 6**  A Sense of Place and Belonging — 100

*Conclusion* — 119
*Notes* — 120
*List of Sources* — 128
*Select Bibliography* — 129
*Index* — 132

# PREFACE

I have always wanted to touch the past, delve deeper into what the documents can tell us to get a sense of who our ancestors were, what they lived through and what they were thinking. I started with the study of archaeology, where I could hold objects of the past in my hand. But I wanted to know more. I then progressed through and undertook a Masters degree in English Local History and delved into family history. It is there I found a way to both touch the past and get a sense of it. One of the best ways to do this was looking at what our ancestors purposely left behind: their gravestone or monument. These are pieces (in my view) of living archaeology; they are what our ancestors wanted to leave behind and were left by both the living and the dead. The aim of this book is to show how much information can be gained from the study of gravestones and how the information present can be used to further and enhance genealogical and family history research. Gravestones offer a wide range of information available to the local and family historian and genealogist, from the usual names and dates through to details that are not recorded anywhere else. In this book I explore gravestones with the underlying theme of identity, and look at the ways in which people – both the living and the dead – have portrayed their identity, and societal beliefs, on their own gravestones and monuments, as well as those of family members. I investigate the symbolism of the images used, the dedications to the deceased, with the switch from corpses to remembrance, to the biographical details they leave such as place, occupations, family ties, wills, and even how they died. These are all things that we associate with our identity.

I have taken examples of individual gravestones for each chapter and made little case studies of them to show how the graves and the historical documents especially the local newspapers of the times, can work hand in hand together to build a bigger picture of how our ancestors lived and died. Throughout the book I have transcribed the stones as they are written with the abbreviations and differences in spelling as these subtle differences can give us a sense of the times in which they lived.

# PICTURE CREDITS

The photographs and maps that follow in this book were taken or drawn by the author, with the following exceptions: The Commonwealth War Graves from Heacham Norfolk, and the Mort Safes from Greyfriars Kirkyard, Edinburgh, which were kindly taken, and permission for use given, by Mrs Carol Brown. The historical documents pictured are referenced and accessed through findmypast.com and ancestry.com.

# ACKNOWLEDGEMENTS

I would like to thank Mrs Carol Brown for her help with taking photographs and for accompanying me round the churchyards in Norfolk. To the kind volunteers in the churches, who have helped with little bits of information and pointing out gravestones and memorials as I have wandered around the churches and churchyards with my notebook and camera on numerous occasions. Finally, to my husband Thomas Leedham who has given his continuous and unwavering support throughout this project, especially when on numerous occasions I have bent his ear off talking about gravestones! He has given me the motivation and the confidence and endless cups of tea to bring this all together. Without his love and support it would have been so much harder.

# LIST OF ABBREVIATIONS

| | |
|---|---|
| LRO | Leicestershire Record Office |
| OED | Oxford English Dictionary. |
| VCH | Victoria County Histories |
| CWGC | Commonwealth War Graves Commission |
| ATS | Auxiliary Territorial Service |
| JP | Justice of the Peace |

# INTRODUCTION

Everyone dies. It is the one thing in life that is certain to happen. Our ancestors may not have got married or baptised, had the best job, or been rich and famous. But they were all buried in some way.

Through tracing our family history, we are on the adventure of trying to find out where we come from, how our identity originated and through whom. The OED describes Identity as who or what a person, or thing is. A set of characteristics or a description that distinguishes a person or thing from others. Everyone has an identity in life; a sense of individuality, morals, our own choices, and things that make us who we are. But when we die is this sense of identity lost? Do our gravestones and memorials portray who we were in life or what we did?

On modern gravestones the only form of identity (other than our name) to have stood the test of time is our association with family. There are still family plots and family gravestones. However, in society today we have different ways to preserve the identity of the deceased, and one of those is by putting a photograph of that person on the gravestone. This is one of the ultimate ways of preserving the identity of a person long after the direct descendants have passed. For our ancestors this type of commemoration would have been reserved for the very rich, with monumental marble carvings or death masks. But never on a gravestone in the churchyard.

I have been very fortunate that my genealogical and family history research has led me to spend many days wandering around churches and churchyards across the breadth of the country, in the hope of discovering a hidden gem of information upon a grave marker. I have looked at thousands of stones and memorials, both inside churches and in the churchyards, and recorded over 2,000 of them. These are mostly from the ancient parish churches of the city of Leicester and surrounding county, villages in Devon, Lincolnshire, Norfolk and east Northumberland, as this is where the bulk of my research has been based. The stones range from the seventeenth century right through to the twentieth. The largest number of graves, as you might expect, date from the eighteenth and nineteenth centuries. Leicester and the surrounding county have a rather unique position in that most of the gravestones are made from Swithland and Groby slate. This is far more durable than sandstone or limestone which is used in many other areas of the country, especially Norfolk and Lincolnshire, and as a result a great many of the stones survive in good condition. However, just because it *can* survive it doesn't mean it *has*, nor that it was even left for us to find.

The eighteenth century saw the start of the graveyard boom by the new up and coming lower-middle and middle classes. The upper classes had been burying their dead inside churches for centuries as they could afford to pay for lavish tombs and family vaults. With the rise of the middle class came the development of the gravestone. This was supposedly done to emulate the upper classes and enhance their social status. However, the stones were nothing like the ones that the upper classes constructed and many of the middle classes had their own ideas and values that they wanted to portray. Some of these memorials started out as freestanding headstones or flat slabs with virtually no biographical information on them at all, sometimes not even a full name and just initials present. The person that is memorialised by these stones has no identity; we do not even know their name. There are stones like this present in most churchyards. Some are on their own but many of them I have found are situated at the back or to the side of later, larger stones. Does this mean that they are family relatives? Are they grave markers for the larger headstones, to mark who is buried and where to erect a permanent feature? Perhaps a larger headstone was never produced for those that were on their own. Unfortunately, we will never know the true answer.

There are problems when researching gravestones regardless of their material. There is the natural wear and tear of the stones from the elements, but also graveyard disturbance, breakages and vandalism, and the movement of the stones all together. The latter instances are especially prevalent with major cities up and down the country as they continue to grow and expand. A large portion of this is due to making the old churches and churchyards accessible to both people and vehicles, especially in the inner cities.

For people to write something in stone is a permanent act and is something either that the deceased wanted people to see, or reflects how the surviving relatives wanted them to be seen, such as a 'doting wife' or 'loving husband'. In some cases, this may be the only surviving primary source left of that individual, or evidence that they even existed at all. The information that is left on the gravestones and monuments can also give us the opportunity to explore further into the lives of our ancestors by using newspapers and other primary sources that may not be the norm, which I have done where possible.

Not all the elements I discuss are present on every stone, but each one gives us a glimpse into how that person wanted to be remembered, the society in which they lived and died, and the beliefs of those left behind – because one vital thing that you need to remember when researching gravestones is that the dead do not bury themselves.

# PRACTICALITIES OF RESEARCHING GRAVESTONES

One of the best things about researching gravestones and monuments is that you do not need any specialist equipment. Most churchyards are open to the public during daylight hours even if the church is not. The only time that I have come across a closed churchyard is when the churchyard itself is unsafe. However, there are few things to note and that makes researching easier. Some churchyards have been left to go back to nature or are no longer maintained, which can make it difficult for researchers to view the stones. This can be the case especially where there are no longer interments, or when the church is no longer in regular use. This can sometimes mean nettles or brambles, so I would recommend long trousers and gloves!

The equipment that I use for recording gravestones ranges from the basic notebook and pencil for noting names, dates and sketches, to charcoal and tracing paper and of course a camera. In society today most of us have access to (usually in our pockets or bag) a mobile phone which has a note-making facility and a camera. If you are new to researching gravestones, this is all you really need to start recording them.

However, during my research I have tried many techniques to record gravestones, especially if the churchyard is not one that I may be able to return too. Depending on whether I am researching a particular family or the whole churchyard, I have a slightly different approach. If it is a particular family or family group, I head straight for that area if known and make a detailed plan of those graves: how many there are, where they are in the churchyard, and if there are any defining features to that area or the stones. If I am researching the whole churchyard then I take a photograph of the information board for the church and start at the entrance gate of the churchyard and work my way around. I use the gate as a marker and write down whether I turn left or right and what style the graves are laid out in, whether in plots, straight lines, side by side, back-to-back, or random placements. This helps to decipher if they have been moved previously and if they have been moved between your visits (and yes, this can happen and has happened to me).

Recording the stones themselves is a personal preference. I like to take photographs and make physical notes there and then, rather than just photograph them and make notes later. I do this for a few reasons; the first is that a photograph may not capture everything that the stones have to offer up-close, such as the feel of the stone, whether there is any part that is submerged or covered in moss/grass, and you cannot always get a sense of size. I tend to use my own height as reference as I am only 5ft (150cms), I note down if it is taller than me or half my height etc. The second is that due to the different types of stone, erosion or damage, you may not always be able to read all – or any – of the information present, but this is where the photographs come in handy. I always photograph these stones, because I can then later play with the contrast and the black-and-white colouring of the image, which can then help to reveal the different shadows the carvings present, which might not have been decipherable with the naked eye. This can also be achieved by tracing paper and either chalk/wax crayons like a brass rubbing. However, this is not always practical, especially if the gravestone is sandstone or limestone as the last thing that you want to do is damage it further.

There are also a few good primary source websites that can also aid in your research; www.findagrave.com is one that I frequently visit. This has lots of images of gravestones from across the country, listed by church. These are taken by members of the public and volunteers so the amount available for each church varies. But because they might have been taken at different times of day and the year to your own pictures, they could have evidence of stones that were no longer visible when you visited. Some of the images also have a transcription of the stone too which can be helpful. But a note of caution with this: I would always recommend you look at the image yourself and not rely on transcriptions alone as this is an interpretation of the text by another person and human error is always a possibility. This website is free to view and search and is also available through ancestry.com.

Deceased online (www.deceasedonline.com) is another website that has a wealth of information from scanned primary documents to photographs of monuments and grave location plot maps. This is a site that you must pay for, and it has various ways and subscription options to do this. However, it is free to search their database to see if they have what you are looking for.

The Commonwealth War Graves Commission website (www.cwgc.org) is also a fantastic source for graves and memorials from the world wars. It is a free site that offers images, primary sources and information regarding the memorials and gravestones.

Local historical and archaeological societies can also offer a wide range of information for the churches and churchyards in their areas and sometimes primary images for your research.

As with all primary sources spelling of names, ages and dates may not be what you expect, or differ from other sources. Just because it is (literally) set in stone does not mean that it is 100 per cent correct. The stonemasons still rely on relatives, or whoever is commissioning the stone or monument, to provide the information, and to use their own judgement when creating the headstone. As with marriage registers, census records etc, there can be differences with the spelling of names, dates and other details due to human error, misinformation and perhaps illiteracy. However, even taking all this into account, gravestones are a great place to start.

*Chapter 1*

# SYMBOLISM, WORDING AND BELIEFS

Images and dedications are present on nearly all gravestones. Each has a dramatic effect on the way that the person or persons are seen and remembered, giving them a form of identity in death. They can also shed light on the feelings and the beliefs of society at the time of burial. The images that people leave and the language that they used to commemorate the dead has changed dramatically over the years. Why did this happen? What happened, or was happening, in the lives at that time for the living to change the way the dead were commemorated?

There are many different types and styles of images and statements that appear on the stones in churchyards and on larger memorials inside churches. However, it does not matter if it is a large marble memorial on the wall of the church, or a small carving in the corner of a headstone in the churchyard. A picture can say a thousand words and it can be interpreted differently by every onlooker. We will never know the true meaning behind every image that is carved, or the thought behind the statements; however, I will try and give an interpretation of the images and the possible reasoning behind the statements.

**Symbolism**

The marking of burials with stones and pictures has been happening since the prehistoric period. Neolithic people built long barrows with large stones and Bronze Age people built round barrows and covered them in white chalk to make them stand out for all to see that this was a place for the dead – and more importantly, ancestors. The ideas and practices have been changed and adapted by generations of ancestors, but the essence of marking a place for, or of, the dead stayed the same,

*Buried gravestone, St Nicholas churchyard Leicester.*

culminating in the gravestones and monuments that we have today. As you might expect, the images that are displayed on the walls on the inside of the churches are better preserved than those outside because they are not open to the elements. Many of the memorials inside churches are carved in marble, alabaster, or cast in metal such as brass, and are generally more expensive than the graves on the outside. These are usually commissioned by the higher-ranking members of the community. However, this does not imply that the meanings behind the images are different.

Symbols and dedications usually appear on the top of the stones and in some cases are the only part of the stone left showing after the passage of time, as was the case at St Nicholas churchyard Leicester. Therefore, knowing what the images mean and the thinking behind the dedications can help family and local historians have a sense of what was happening at the time of burial and when that might have been.

## Images of Mortality and Remembrance

The pictures that have been carved on stones have changed over time. The ones that are on seventeenth- and eighteenth-century stones are predominately images of mortality.

The most common image of mortality (as you would probably imagine) is the skull. This has been used on its own, as skull and cross bones, as a whole skeleton, or alongside other symbols of mortality. These include, but are not exclusive too, the grim reaper or a scythe the harvester of

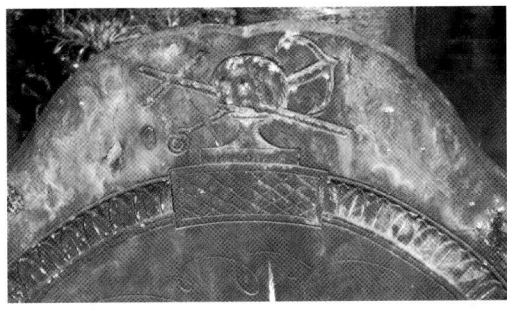

*Gravestone, skull with cross and anchor from St Mary De Castro churchyard Leicester.*

*Scene of Mortality on gravestone from St Margaret's churchyard Leicester.*

*Images of mortality from St John the Baptist churchyard, Grimston Leicestershire.*

*Temptations of the world from St Mary De Castro churchyard Leicester.*

*Hourglass, Skulls, Sextons' tools on gravestone from St Martin's churchyard Leicester.*

souls; coffins and sextons' tools for burial; an hourglass or father of time to represent the passing of time and life; wings for the fleetingness of life.

The images show the elaborate ways that people have used symbols to depict mortality. The image from St Margaret's churchyard Leicester, shows death handing the dying person the temptations of the world. Also, an image from St Mary De Castro churchyard Leicester, showing depictions of the skull and the skeleton in a coffin. Many of the images of death and bones are accompanied with the phrase 'Memento Mori', which is Latin for 'remember you must die'. Although these are rather gruesome images, they are not as macabre as we might consider them today, because they were people's reality of death.

These images are depicted during a time when there seems to be an obsession with death, and given that life expectancy was around forty-five years old it is not surprising. Death was commonplace, with many periodical outbreaks of plague and other illnesses which only ceased after the mid-seventeenth century, but were then succeeded by epidemics of smallpox and cholera, not forgetting the appalling living conditions of the lower classes. Death was all around, so it is not surprising that there are many depictions of it.

The uses of images of mortality slowly began to disappear at the start of the nineteenth century and when they did still appear they were a lot more discreet; you would not know they were there if you were not looking for them. The emphasis of the images was now on mourning. There was a big increase in the number of women and children appearing on the stones. The weeping lady and hope and anchor appear in all the churchyards. One of the reasons for this (which will be discussed in more detail later in the chapter) is that death was not seen as scary anymore and there is more emphasis on the remembrance of the deceased and the mourner's loss rather than the decaying body.

The image that is found most frequently both inside and outside of the church is the urn. I have noted over 127 different styles of urns that are carved on the memorials; some are draped, others are not, some are very large and dominate, others are very small and simple. They appear in nearly all the time periods that I have looked at. The urn was used from the early to mid-1700s right through to the twentieth century. It has been adapted and changed to suit each person's perceptions of death or remembrance and has stood the test of time. The thing that is quite strange is that the real meaning of the urn is not known. Today, the accepted meaning is that it is a Greek symbol of mourning symbolising the body as a vessel for the soul.[1] It is also a possibility that the urn was simply the easiest, or cheapest, thing for the stonemason to carve.

# Symbolism, Wording and Beliefs

*Various types and styles of urns on gravestones.*

*Early cherubs from 1700s St John the Baptist, Grimston, Leicestershire.*

Urns appear most often at the top of gravestones. There are instances where an urn covers the whole top of the stone, and others as just a small depiction; sometimes they are combined with large images of mortality as we have seen above, others with very subtle ones such as just the word 'mortality' written beneath it. Occasionally it will be used to support other figures such as a weeping lady.

The image of the cherub is present in all the churchyards. Although not as abundant as you might have expected in the inner-city churchyards, it is far more common in rural churchyards such as in the village of Grimston in Leicestershire, and in villages of Snettisham and Dersingham in Norfolk. The most popular form of cherub I have come across is that of a childlike human head and large wings. The cherub traditionally signified that the soul had gone to heaven. It has (and still does) often marked the grave of a child guarding its soul on the journey to heaven. They can be found in pairs or on their own, and are sometimes associated with other images – sometimes of mortality, others of remembrance and resurrection. However, the actual carving of the cherub itself can vary depending on the year and the stonemason.

*Cherubs and other symbols from All Saints' churchyard Leicester.*

Cherubs have been pictured with other symbolic images such as the hourglass, book and torch. The hourglass is seen as a symbol of mortality with the passing of time, the book and the torch may symbolise knowledge and life. Cherubs have also been pictured with images of skulls.

These are images that you would possibly expect to find in churchyards, however, the stones reveal some images you may not expect, or we are very unsure of their meaning nowadays. There is an image of Jack of Green, or the Green Man, on a stone in St Nicholas churchyard. He has different names depending on where you are in the country.

This image has been around since the Roman period and can be found in many medieval churches.[2] The image today is generally associated

*Jack of Green, St Nicholas churchyard Leicester.*

with life and renewal, and the Green Man is celebrated on May Day with parades through the streets in towns such as Hastings. However, the meaning behind it has been the subject of some dispute. Kathleen Basford believes the Green Man to be a more sinister image representing a thing of sorrow,[3] and she has looked at the work carried out by Betty Wilsher on Scottish gravestones where the image is associated with mortality.[4] However, she does recognise that an image can change its meaning over time and that we do not always have to agree on a certain meaning.[5] It will be hard to determine why it was put on the stone with no other images at all to sway the argument. However, in my view the symbol represents life and rebirth, which is what the Green Man represents.

There are also what look like religious scenes recreated on the stones, but these are far fewer than I imagined at the start. The ones I have come across are present in the sandstone graves of Dersingham and Snettisham churchyards in Norfolk.

However, the use of the letters I.H.S, which are the first three letters in Greek of the name Jesus, are very frequent.[6] Although there are some images that have been associated with religion, they very often appear

*Religious scene on gravestone from the churchyard of St Mary's church Snettisham Norfolk.*

with other images, some of them relating to mortality, which could give them a different meaning. Some of the stones have images of books and crowns. These are not on their own and are always with other images on the stones. The meaning of the crown has been described as symbol of honour or glory and its usual sense refers to Paul's metaphor to the Corinthians (I. Cor. 9:24-27) to the immortal crown of Christian life.[7] The book on the other hand does not have an exact meaning; it is possible that it could signify a prayer book, but it could also signify knowledge. The interpretation of this image is down to the person looking at it and any other symbols it is with.

There are big differences in the way that these images are presented inside the church to how they are outside, and they can give a certain feel to the inside of the church. As you walk around the inside of St Martin's Church, now Leicester Cathedral, and St Mary De Castro Church Leicester, St Wilfrid's Church, Alford, Lincolnshire, St Mary's Church, Appledore, Devon, there is a sense of awe and wonder at these fantastically large and dominating memorials, they certainly give a grand impression and show the wealth of certain people in the respective parishes. However, this is not true of all churches, this is the very opposite to that of All Saints' Church and St Nicholas Church Leicester, which had very few elaborate images on the walls and in the churchyard too. This gives the impression that these parishes were much poorer than the others and the feel inside the church is a little bit calmer, more spiritual if that is possible. St Margaret's Leicester, and St Mary's Snettisham, Norfolk, on the other hand is a mix of the two and have many memorials on the walls, although the interiors are not dominated by them.

The gravestones in the churchyards have some fantastic imagery on them but inside the churches the dominant image is the urn. Rather than the intricate details present on the gravestones however, there seems to be rather more emphasis on the size of the memorial, the writing on it, the material it is made of and, in some cases, carvings of the deceased themselves.

The number of people leaving stone headstones dramatically increased between the seventeenth and nineteenth centuries as the association with the church and burials increased. Previously, if the poorer classes left any grave markers at all, they tended to be wooden, as this is what they could afford; the upper classes would be memorialised in the church itself. However, we can get a feel for the wealth of the parish and its inhabitants by the style and amount of large and highly decorated memorials in the church and outside in the churchyard, as there seems to be a correlation between the number of large memorials inside the church and the wealth of the parish, i.e. the more elaborate and large the memorials, the richer the parish. It would take a skilled craftsman to produce some of the wonderful images that have been produced on the stones and this would have been expensive. However, a written dedication on the top of the stone is something that every stone and memorial has, and it is generally the first thing you see when you are looking at the stones. The language on the top of the stone gives an instant impression of how the deceased saw themselves in death, or the way that the relatives saw them. It gives them an identity, either of being a decaying body or a remembered soul. Those two themes are what are going to be discussed here, as they change dramatically over time; the aim is to look at why this possibly happened.

## Language

During the seventeenth and eighteenth centuries there were a variety of different dedications: 'hear lyeth the body of', 'here lies the mortal remains of', 'here lies the interred the body of', 'here deposited are the remains of', 'near this spot lie the remains of', 'in this vault are the bodies of', 'below is the corpse of'. All these dedications have one thing in common; they are focused on the body or the corpse of the person in the ground. It is about the mortality of the person as an individual and not the people that are mourning their loss. They are also acknowledging that the body is decaying and that they are marking where this is, which gives a great importance to the stone that has been erected.[8] During the middle of the eighteenth century the language starts to change; there is a decrease in the amount of dedications to the body as a corpse, and statements of 'to the memory', and 'in memory of', start to appear alongside the dedications of mortality. Then as the century turns there is a great change in the language, there are very few mortality dedications being left, the emphasis now is upon remembrance. They change to statements such as 'sacred to memory of', 'in affectionate remembrance to', and 'in loving memory'. These are the types of statements that people are used to seeing on gravestones on our memorials today. But why were they buried with language of mortality in the first place and what sparked the change? What happened to cause this great shift in belief of how a person should be commemorated and be identified from a rotting corpse buried in the ground to the remembrance of the person?

*Graves showing change in dedications, St Mary De Castro churchyard Leicester.*

During the seventeenth and much of the eighteenth century, death was more visible and omnipresent, mortality rates were high and life expectancy was very low. Death was not the taboo that it is seen to be today. It was out there in the open as people usually died at home surrounded by family, and it was very common for children to be exposed to death at a very early age. People did not die on their own in a hospital like they do today. Sarah Tarlow has suggested that seventeenth-century monuments show the grizzly fate of the body because they believed that the body is separate from that of the soul and that a person's essence was not tied to their corporeal form and therefore the dead body is represented as waste matter destined to be worm food.[9] I believe that there is more to it.

This was an era where disease and epidemics were rife and in the poorer areas of our large cities and towns there was vast overcrowding and acceptable sanitation was next to none. There were outbreaks of smallpox, cholera and tuberculosis, these diseases were horrific, and people were witness to this. It is also common in poorer families to keep the body of the deceased in the house for a week or more in order for the family to have time to raise the cash for burial, even with a contagious disease.[10] Also, in the poorer families the usual day for burial would have been a Sunday, as any other day in the week would have resulted in a loss of earnings.[11] This meant that the body could possibly stay in the house for longer than a week, and depending on the time of year it is very likely that the body would start to decompose.

It was not just due to the practicality of the cost of the burial however, families also had a ritual that meant that the body was kept in the house. It was called watching the dead. This ritual can be dated back to the fourteenth century where the body was watched for the entire duration from death to burial.[12] In wealthier families that kept this tradition, the body would have been placed in a separate room from the living quarters and then watched by members of the family. In poorer families, even if they did not keep this tradition, in the overcrowded houses it is very possible that the body would have been in the same room that everyone lived in, and in some cases the deceased might occupy the only bed until funds were raised to pay for burial.[13] With this it is not surprising that the dedications were of mortality and bodies, as this is what people saw. The poem *Elegy Written in a County Churchyard* written in the eighteenth century by Thomas Gray, also gives a good idea of the way that people saw death and burial through the language that he uses. The poem is about what the people in the churchyard will not see again and he uses words such as 'cold ear of death', 'bones' and 'mould'ring heap'.[14] Even in this lovely poem there is still evidence of the reality of death as an awful thing.

The watching of the body became more than just a tradition for some people. This was because of the widespread fear (especially in the Victorian period and earlier) of being buried alive and that people wanted to show that the person buried in the ground was the corpse or the remains of that person. Today this sounds such an absurd thing to be afraid of, surely people would know if their relatives were dead or not. However, this does not seem to be the case. During the 1800s it was not the norm for a person to be examined by a physician and declared dead. Doctors, or so-called doctors, would hold mirrors or a glass under the nostrils of the deceased, touch their skin with hot pokers or cut a vein to see if they were really dead. However, this service would have had to be paid for. The only real way to determine whether a person was dead was when they started to decompose. The fear was so bad that there were reports made, and inventions that people could buy or rent, to alert people if this had happened. Welcome, the invention of the safety coffin. This is where a bell, or a flag string, was placed inside the coffin in the hand of the deceased and if it rang or moved then the person was still alive and needed to be rescued. This fear, it would seem, was not as far-fetched as we would think. The newspaper headlines and articles of the time give us an indication of the types of problems and instances that were reported to have occurred.

The *London Evening Standard* on 6 September 1849 reports of 'Cholera Deaths and Inquests', where Mr Brown the milkman of Camden Town, who was supposed to have died from cholera, was buried very speedily and his family from the country were unable to make it in time for his funeral and insisted on seeing the body. On being 'taken up' the body was found on its side in the coffin and his knuckles cut in a 'shocking manner'. It also gives evidence of a lady who was reported to have died from cholera who was buried then hours later found alive.

The *Carlisle Journal* of 28 December 1849 reports: 'Not a few individuals are haunted with the idea of being buried alive. Some women, it is affirmed, will scarcely sleep, lest they awake and find a coffin for a bed.'

It was not just people being buried alive at home that was reported, but instances abroad too. *Derbyshire Advertiser and Journal* of 4 June 1847 reports of cases in France where people had been buried alive and awoke in coffins.

Even Edwin Chadwick in his *Report on Sanitation* had specific sections on premature interment and how to prevent it. He was concerned with the delay of interment and length of time that the body was left in the house. He found that it was not always due to the cost of funerals, which was a great problem for the lower classes as we have seen, but even when the expenses were covered there was still a delay due to the 'fear of interment before life is extinct'.[15] In London in 1869 the London Association for Prevention of Premature Burial was established. Its members were appalled by the lack of laws relating to burial and called for legislation to provide better securities to prevent premature burial.[16]

People were so concerned by the fact that they would be buried before they had died that they left instructions in their wills on what to do in the event of their death. Many of these were published in the newspapers along with their probate when it was proved, and they are not as early as you would expect.

In 1917 the *Times* in London published the probate of Miss Rose Elizabeth Greene under the title '*Afraid of Premature Burial*'. It details her estate but also that she requested in 'her will that her remains be burned at Titchfield Hants but not until a week after her death'.[17]

In 1927 the *Times*, London published the probate of former headteacher Miss Lucy Helen Muriel Soulsby of Reading, who stated in her will that 'Whereas I have always desired every precaution against being buried alive, I desire that at my death the doctor shall cut my carotid artery and if by some mistake this is omitted, I desire that my body be exhumed and this be done.'[18] Both women were spinsters and they wanted control over their death and burial, as they had in life.

In October 1829 the *Weekly Dispatch* in London published the announcement of the proved probate of the Late William Hunt Esquire. Here in this little article we are given a glimpse into his fears – and not just of being buried alive. The newspaper reports that he had 'great anxiety not to be buried alive and also to escape the resurrection men'. It states that attached to the front of his will 'was an advert of a patent self-closing and un-openable iron coffin and his will directs that he is to be buried in iron or stone coffin but not until undoubted signs of putrefaction appear upon his body.'[19]

The other fear that William Hunt Esquire describes which would have influenced the change of wording on dedications was that of grave robbing, dissection and the Anatomy Act of 1832.[20] Before the Anatomy Act was passed the only way that surgeons were able to gain access to bodies for dissection was through the Murder Act of 1752.[21] This only allowed bodies of executed murderers to be used for dissection. However, through the progress of medical science and the reduction in executions there were not enough bodies to satisfy the surgeons' demand, and this led to a rise in body snatching and people known as resurrectionists or resurrection men. The most well-known are Burke and Hare, who operated in Edinburgh, Scotland. However, this atrocity happened across the British Isles. There is a handwritten report from 1825 by the committee of St Margaret's Church Leicester, asking for witnesses to come forward to help them find and convict the person or persons 'who took away the corpse from the churchyard on or about the 14th December last', and they offer a reward of £100 for the capture.[22] This is a vast sum of money for that time period; the RPI for that sum today is about £6,890, and as a southern agricultural labourer would earn about 8 or 9 shillings, the reward money being offered was a large incentive. This shows how important it was for the parish that these people were found, and how they felt about it as they describe the taking of the corpse as a 'horrid practice'.

The newspapers of the period have many details of the ways in which the resurrection men worked and what happened to them when they are caught. The problem was that even though the public condemned them, and if they were caught, found guilty and sentenced to either transportation or imprisonment, the demand for cadavers was fuelling the trade. I found a case in the *London Morning Post* of 21 January 1821, where two gentlemen from the faculty of St Thomas' Hospital, London, where present at the trial of two body-snatchers and posted their bail.[23] It wasn't just the high price surgeons were willing to pay for bodies. There was also the problem that the people behind the body-snatching also thought that what they were doing was a necessity to medical science. This can be seen in the *Drakards Stamford News* of 7 April 1826, with the conviction of William Clark who was accused of stealing four dead bodies from the churchyard of Walcot in Bath. However, it is clear from his confession that William had been plying this trade since the age of 6 and had assisted in procuring over 2,000 bodies and had been tried twenty-eight times for the offence. In his defence 'he urged the necessity of bodies has been for purposes of medical science, and declared that even the King had been benefited by his labour; for when his majesty required an operation, he had obtained four subjects for a preliminary trial'.[24] William was sentenced to a £100 fine and a year's imprisonment.

At the time it was popularly understood that the surgeons' official interest was not to revive but to destroy. Dissection was seen as the final process; it denied any hope of survival from hanging and, so people believed, even the survival of the person's identity after death.[25] This is the part that people were most afraid of. The Anatomy Act 1832 allowed surgeons' access to corpses that were not claimed forty-eight hours after death, particularly those that were in prisons or workhouses.

With people putting the statements 'here lyeth the body of', or 'here lie the remains of', then this could be seen as possible advertisement for the body snatchers as it is factual rather than affectionate. It gives no evidence of people or relatives remembering or claiming the deceased, even though putting up a stone should signify that. However, if people changed the statements to 'in memory of', or 'in remembrance of', then it is possible that they are showing a claim of the body; this is their ancestor, and they want people to know that they are remembered and that they are claimed and that they cannot be taken.

Even with the change in commemoration, the public took many measures to guard themselves from body-snatchers and evidence can be seen of this in churchyards. The most famous one is that of Greyfriars Kirkyard in Edinburgh, Scotland. In this churchyard there are still iron mort safes in situ that were put over the graves to prevent grave robbers accessing the bodies. Mort safes could be rented or purchased from the funeral directors and went over the outside of the grave.

For those who could afford it, as we have seen previously from the will of William Hunt, people could also opt for an iron or stone coffin. There were also other ways that people tried to prevent the bodies being stolen. Coffin collars were placed over the body and screwed to the coffin to prevent the body being dragged out. Also, people tried to render the body useless for dissection by putting quicklime into the coffin to destroy them.[26] There were also a few more extreme ways that were advertised. In the *Weekly Globe*, London in 1829 there was an advert for 'Complete Mode of Preventing Grave Robbing', this was advising using a pistol with powder and ball cocked in the coffin with the string attached to the lid resulting in it going off if tried to be opened.[27]

*Mort Safe grave, Greyfriars Kirkyard, Edinburgh.*

> **BODY SNATCHERS.**
>
> COMPLETE MODE OF PREVENTING GRAVE ROBBING.
>
> Charge a pistol with powder and ball and place it in the coffin alongside the corpse. The pistol must be left cocked and pointing upwards, with a string from the trigger fastened to the inside of the lid of the coffin. Should any attempt be made to rob the grave by breaking the coffin or attempting to force the lid, the pistol will necessarily be snapped and go off, the consequence of which must be fatal to the insurrection-man, who, in such case, should be a perquisite to the parish surgeon, and do the service which he was raising the dead to perform. If it were generally known that this device was adopted in a few cases, this class of robbers would be deterred from their unhallowed pursuits.

Weekly Globe *London, 4 January 1829 British Newspaper Archive.*

Fear of something can be a big instigator when it comes to change but so can hope. One of the most significant things to bring about this change was the advancement in medicine and the area that had the most far-reaching effect was that of pain relief. There was still very little a doctor could do about infectious diseases once they had taken hold, but they could help with the pain. There were ways in which people used to try to ease the pain of death in the early Georgian and Victorian periods with the use of opium, laudanum and alcohol being common – and these were not just restricted to the wealthier classes. Such medicines were available in patent formulas such as Dover's Powders and Godfrey's Cordial. These would give the taker a 'drug death', which could resemble a gentle slipping in to sleep.[28] However, the introduction of ether in 1846 and chloroform in 1847 marked a major advance in the war on pain.[29] Many chemists were administering ether, but it was John Snow MD who put it to the forefront. He devised new and improved ways of administering ether and chloroform. John Snow's most famous patient was Queen Victoria. When Prince Leopold was born on 7 April 1853, Snow administered chloroform to Her Majesty, who expressed herself as greatly relieved by the administration. This occurrence had a profound effect on public opinion.[30] John Snow published many books on ether and chloroform, and these had a major impact on the medical world. Chloroform could produce a deeper anaesthetic state than ether and as a result it was more dangerous; if doctors got it wrong then it was an instant death, so people were still wary of it.

There were many other advances in medicine and sanitation reforms that all helped to change the way that people saw death. John Snow did great work in London on the cholera epidemics. He found a link to the water pumps and published many papers on the prevention of cholera.[31] There was also the smallpox vaccination, which brought hope to many and saw the beginnings of the disease being eradicated, and Edwin Chadwick's 1842 report on the sanitary conditions of the labouring population of Great Britain showed that unsanitary conditions were one of the main causes of disease. Both topics are covered in more detail in the chapter on child mortality.

As the Victorian period progressed so did the advances in medicine and this saw a permanent change in the way that death was seen. The doctor became a prominent feature of the deathbed scene, and as things continued to improve and hospitals were able to prevent and cure illnesses, life expectancy increased, and death became more associated with old age. This is shown in an article in the *London Fortnightly Review* of 1899, which stated that death had 'lost its terror'.[32] These changes to the way that the deceased are memorialised, from a rotting corpse to a remembered soul, are ones that we still use today. Death, or more specifically the physicality of death, is something that is not spoken about unless there is a particular reason, such as a terminal illness. It is not the norm for people to be associated with a dead body on a regular basis, as was the case for our ancestors; today, this is left to professionals in hospitals and funeral directors and so the detail is not shown on the grave monuments. There certainly would not be any mention of decomposing remains. It is the identity of the dead as a living person that is now at the forefront, and even if there are no other details of the deceased mentioned, they are still remembered.

*Chapter 2*

# CHILDREN, FAMILY AND ANCESTORS

The identity of the infants and children that are buried in churchyards is harder to determine than those of adults. Today, children are buried in their own areas of cemeteries or churchyards surrounded by other children. These stones are often smaller in size and have images that relate to children, such as teddy bears to depict that this was a young child. During the seventeenth, eighteenth and nineteenth centuries this was not the case. Here, I am going to discuss the way that children have been memorialised and why those actions were taken. It is also going to look at the family dynamic, the way that family members are memorialised on the stones, the differences between men and women, and with whom people identify themselves with.

### Children's burials

We know from historical documents such as the census and parish baptism records, that our ancestors tended to have large families with many children. Unfortunately, we also know that many did not survive. But the documents can only tell us so much, depending on how long the child lived and the family's social class. This is where the gravestones can help. The identity of children has been displayed in several ways. In some cases, the child or children have their own stone. These are generally the same size and shape as an adult stone with their name, age at death, and even other biographical information such as when they were born. These types of stones can be seen up and down the country.

An example of this can be seen in St Nicholas churchyard Leicester. The gravestone is dedicated to the children of John and Catherine Bradley.

> 'To the memory of William and Catherine children of John
> and Catherine Bradley
> William died Feby 24th 1792 aged 3 months
> Catherine April 1797 aged 3 years'

It states the children's names, who their mother and father were and the dates and ages they were when they died. The stone is rather plain with no ornate stonework. However, a stone from St Mary De Castro churchyard Leicester, is slightly different. The stone commemorates a single child.

> 'Charles the son of Thomas and Sarah Smith who died Jan 9th 1820,
> aged 5 years and 10 months'.

This gravestone depicts who his parents were, the date when he died, and his age. The memorial, however, is more elaborate than the one from St Nicholas churchyard as it has a decorative urn on top with a skull in it surrounded by roses and has a sentimental passage at the bottom. The reason for this could be that Charles was older than William and Catherine when he died. Or more likely of circumstance, because the parish of St Nicholas was in the poorer part of the city and the parents of Charles were probably wealthier and could afford a more elaborate memorial for him.

There is also a gravestone in St Margaret's churchyard Leicester, where five children are commemorated.

> 'In memory of five children of Richard and Elizabeth Rawson. Henry Rawson died 1802 aged 2 years Bertie Rawson died 1806 aged 5 years John Charles Rawson died 1817 aged 8 Jessica Rawson 1817 aged 15 Robert Rawson died 1818 aged 22 years'.

Unfortunately gravestones like this one, depicting more than one child, are a common occurrence in many churchyards and churches. The reasons for this will be looked at later in the chapter. However, it is not just young children that are commemorated as the wall memorial inside Holy Trinity Church Tattershall Lincolnshire shows:

> 'Near the north door are interred the remains of John Marston Surgeon
> For nearly thirty years an active and skilled practitioner at Tattershall in
> the county died Decr 30th 1839 aged 50 years
> Also Elizabeth Chettle his wife departed this life Novr 16th 1836 aged 53

> *Also the undermentioned children of the above John and Elizabeth C*
> *Mary Anne died Aug 9th 1835 aged 22*
> *Eliza died Feby 2nd 1838 aged 22*
> *Sophia died Jany 6th 1838 aged 20*
> *Catherine died Dec 29th 1839 aged 21*
> *Stephan died 9th Oct 1837 aged 15*
> *Also George died Apr 24th 1830 aged 15 interred at Tattershall with three children who died infants*
> *Thomas 9th son died Decr 24th 1843 aged 22'*

Generally, this is the way that most children were memorialised – on the stones of relatives. The most common relatives, as you would expect, is that of either their mother or father. The usual way that the children appear is by being named at the bottom of the stone. This can be seen in St John the Baptist churchyard, Grimston, where there is a stone dedicated to John Gamble, his wife Sarah, and their children Mary, Edward and Thomas. The children are at the bottom of the stone. The same can be seen from many other churchyards where it is the parents who are commemorated and then at the bottom it states 'also', and then the name of the child and when they died. Grandparents may also have their grandchildren written on the bottom of their stone. This occurs in All Saints' churchyard Leicester where the grandparents have died only a few years before their granddaughter, and they have had their granddaughter commemorated on their stone.

> 'Sacred to the memory of Jonah Fossett who departed this life 20th Jan 1814 aged 69 years Also Ann wife of Jonah Fossett who died May 21st 1822 aged 77 years, Likewise Ann Elizabeth Fossett granddaughter of above who died 6th June 1820 aged 11 months'.

The identity of the children commemorated on these stones is still very clear, they are remembered as people. However, this is not the case for all.

## Infant Mortality

The representation of dead infants on gravestones is unfortunately one of the most frequent findings during the eighteenth and nineteenth century. During these centuries Leicester's infant mortality rate was one of the highest in the country. In a report written by the Health of Towns Commission showing the rate of death per 1,000; Leicester's was thirty, which is very high, being exceeded only by Bristol (thirty-one),

Manchester (thirty-two), and Liverpool (thirty-five).[1] This statistic can be clearly seen in all the churchyards but not with the same biographical details as with older children. The way that infants have been depicted varies greatly, but the most frequent is *'Also three children who died in infancy'*, this can also be written as *'died in minority'*. There are very few who have names present and even fewer that have any other biographical information. These depictions are usually found right at the bottom of the stone.

There are hundreds of stones and memorials from inside churches and churchyards I have visited across the country which state that their children died in infancy, and these are the ones we can still see. What is alarming (although not surprising) is the number of children from each family that are being commemorated this way. Less than half of the children are memorialised on their own. There are cases of three, four and five children dying in infancy, and in St Mary De Castro's churchyard Leicester, there is the stone of William Christian who died in 1825 and his wife Sarah who died 1808, and at the bottom of their stone it states, *'Also six of their children'*. These are phenomenal figures to see on gravestones and memorials, and it is not something that as a society we are familiar with today. However, even this small mention can have a big impact for the family historian as this might be the only evidence that the child ever existed. There is no doubt that there are probably many more infants and children that have been memorialised this way that have now been lost to the elements, submerged, or moved, so we may never know how many were commemorated without any real identity and the little bit the child did have is now gone.

But why were parents commemorating their children in this way? One of the main reasons would be cost. During the eighteenth century the usual charge for cutting letters was 1d. per letter.[2] There was also the cost of the stone and the church fees. Many parents could not afford to do this for every child and so used their own or a relative's gravestone to commemorate them as this was more cost effective. Parents would do anything to escape having to place their children in pauper graves. This is where the coffin and the funeral are paid for under the Poor Law Act 1834.[3] However, the deceased would be placed in a simple coffin and in a communal grave with no personal details of any of the individuals buried there. This then led to the stigma of pauperisation of the father, which was a societal disgrace on top of the grief of losing a child. The pauper funeral is also seen as undignified and disrespectful.[4] Many infants who died before baptism, which was usually within a month of birth, were buried without ceremony and put in someone else's grave.[5] There seems to be a clear distinction between the ages when a child gets named on a stone, or when they are just stated as an infant. One of the youngest and earliest children's graves I have found named is Richard Mansfield who is '*3 months 3 weeks and four dayes*'. He is commemorated on a floor slab inside Saint Margaret's Church Leicester.

During the eighteenth and nineteenth century, 'infancy' is generally recognised as between birth and 1 year old, and then a 'child' is usually defined as 1 to 5 years. It is possible that if the child died very soon after birth the family did not have time to formally name them and therefore would not have put the name on the gravestone. That is another reason why they may not have had a grave of their own, because they were not accorded the full status of a person.[6] So the small commemoration on the gravestone may be the only form of identity that the infant has, especially if they were not recorded in the historical records.

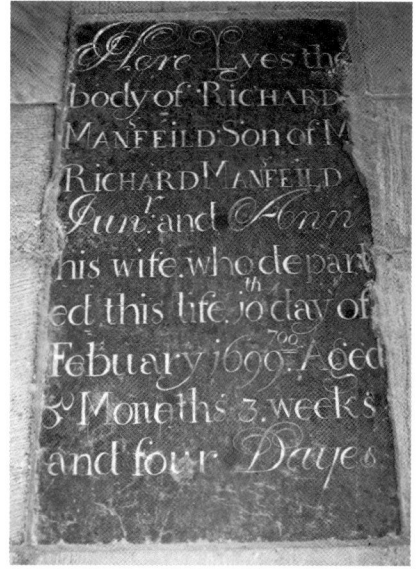

*Floor slab of Richard Mansfield, St Margaret's church Leicester.*

## Why?

What can these dedications to the hundreds of children and infants that died tell us of the society in which our ancestors lived? What happened during the eighteenth and nineteenth centuries to cause these quite dramatic numbers of infant and children's deaths, and why was the mortality rate for Leicester and in other cities so high? It has been stated above that Leicester was one of the unhealthiest places in the country. This is due to it being 'situated in a water-logged valley through which runs the river Soar, probably the most sluggish in its flow of any of the rivers in Great Britain, with its population growing too rapidly for its sanitary arrangements.'[7] This consequence led to overcrowding, poor drainage, and flooding, which altogether was not the answer to a healthy way to live. This is also true for many of the industrial cities such as Manchester, Liverpool and London, to name just a few.

Babies are born with very immature immune systems. They must rely on immunity given to them at the time they are in the womb, and then through breastfeeding. This means that they have a harder time overcoming the stresses that would have only a very mild effect on a mature person.[8] Therefore, if the mother was malnourished or sick due to bad sanitation, living conditions or lack of food, then the infant would also suffer. Weaning was another time when the infants were most vulnerable. If they were weaned off breast milk at a time of year when the bacteria were multiplying rapidly then they were at risk of an infection they would not be able to fight off. This is because cows' milk is not a perfect substitute for breast milk, and during the eighteenth and nineteenth centuries infants could not cope with the impurities found in cows' milk and this resulted in diarrhoea,[9] one of the contributing factors to the high mortality rate.

Diarrhoea was not the only thing that infants, children and the population of Leicester and other industrial cities had to deal with. There were many other diseases and epidemics that swept through, and none more severe than smallpox. Leicester had many periods where smallpox hit the city; one of the most severe cases was that of 1872. What made this case of smallpox more unbearable for the people of Leicester was that most children had been vaccinated against the disease when they were born. Vaccinations started with 74 per cent of children in 1849 being vaccinated at birth, and then rose steadily to its maximum in 1872. Unfortunately, many of the children and adults who had been vaccinated against smallpox died from it.[10] As a result, the people of Leicester distrusted the vaccination and turned to other ways to prevent smallpox and other diseases.

I have found evidence from a stone in St Margaret's churchyard Leicester, that a family died from smallpox. The stone is dedicated to William Curtis and his wife Sarah:

*'To the memory of William Curtis and Sarah his wife both from Tugby in this county and while discharging offices of parental affectionin* [word unreadable] *the afflictions of a daughter fell of smallpox of which they died. He the 20th Oct 1798 aged 66 She the 21st Oct 1798 aged 63'*

They died within a day of each other. This stone gives us a glimpse into the way that this disease can sweep through a family. This family and many generations before would not have had the option of a vaccination, as it was in 1798 that Edward Jenner first published his findings that cow pox could be used to treat smallpox.

There were many issues in Leicester and other cities that had to be addressed with regards to poor sanitation as this, we know today, is one of the main causes for disease. This is especially true for cholera which first appeared in England in the early 1830s. It was a deadly and highly contagious disease which could kill within days. However, during the nineteenth century people thought that disease was carried by bad smells in the air (miasma)[11] and not through water. Leicester had a very inadequate water supply, and was without a piped water supply until 1853. Previously, the water had been taken from wells and cisterns, with the wells in the central market place being fed by a lead conduit, built in 1645, which took fresh water from a spring in St Margaret's parish. However, the water from the well and the conduit was contaminated because of seepage from the cesspits and privies that had been dug down to the water seam.[12] Edwin Chadwick's *'Report on the Sanitary Conditions of Labouring Population of Great Britain'* conducted in July 1842 looked at fifty towns' and cities' poorer areas. The report emphasised the fact that unsanitary conditions were one of the main causes of disease.[13] However, it was not until the Public Health Act of 1848, which gave local authorities the power to appoint Boards of Health, that things started to change. There was, however, opposition to this Act as it meant councils having to spend money. Leicester, unlike other cities, set to work straight away, and by the end of 1849 it was already dealing effectively with such nuisances as pigsties within the town and defective drains and cesspools.[14] This paved the way for what is known as the Leicester method. Along with good sanitation, Leicester isolated, quarantined and disinfected houses that had inhabitants with smallpox, and they were taken to hospital. Leicester managed to prevent smallpox epidemics and other diseases happening again. Leicester's method was to wash and be clean.[15] This can be seen in a report by John Moore *'A Report on the sanitary condition of Leicester in 1860'*. John Moore was the Officer for Health and a Surgeon in the city of Leicester. The report describes the results of the hard work that Leicester had put in which showed that deaths had decreased by over 200 since the previous year, and only two people had died of smallpox.[16] By 1910 Leicester had raised its sanitation level from being one of the unhealthiest large manufacturing towns to one of the healthiest in the country.

It is beyond our capacity to empathise with the families of dead children of any age unless we have experienced it for ourselves. However, even though mortality rates were high, this did not annul the hope that one's child would live. Leicester did have one of the highest infant mortality rates for a time, but a great many children survived, and this is what the parents would have been clinging on to.

**Family**
Family relations are the most common forms of identity on the gravestones and can be so helpful for family historians. We still have family gravestones and plots today. This can be with a mother and father for children, husband and wife, niece or nephew, or grandparents. It was very common in the eighteenth and nineteenth centuries for entire families to be commemorated on the same stone, often with many years between them.

On a family stone the male name usually appears on the top of the stone if the inscriptions go down, or on the left-hand side if written side-by-side. This is reaffirming that even in death the male is head of the family. During the eighteenth and nineteenth century the family or household had a master who was the formal decision maker, the contractual leader entitled to meet out rewards or punishments. This was then made official with the introduction of the census and this position was called the head of household.[17] There are many stones in the churchyards that show the progression of the family. However, there are many that have not been completed; they are either missing a husband, father, wife, or mother. It is clear to see who is missing just by looking at which part of the stone is blank.

It is not uncommon to have other relatives or people that worked with the family or were a big part of family life written on the stones, but they do seem to have their place. They are usually written on the bottom underneath the main family and depending on whether they were male, or female would be put on the correct side accordingly. It is also very common for second wives to be put on the same stone as the first. This is usually underneath the first wife, and it is stated that they are the man's second wife.

*Left side blank on gravestone St Michael's church, Ingoldisthorpe, Norfolk.*

*Right side at the top blank showing missing wife, All Saints churchyard Leicester.*

This can be seen on a stone from St Mary's churchyard Snettisham, Norfolk

*'In Memory of Elizabeth wife of James Nichols who died November 19 1831 aged 29 years also Elizabeth his second wife who died Dec 18 1857'*
[rest of stone submerged]

The blank sections on the stones leave many questions unanswered. Where are the husbands and wives that are missing buried? Could the family not afford to inscribe the stone, had they fallen on hard times? Did they move away and were buried somewhere else, possibly with another family? These are all questions that we are unable to answer from the stones. However, this is where the records can help as we know potentially where they are not buried and who their relatives were.

Families were not just commemorated on the one stone. They can be seen in family groups in many of the churchyards, where they have the same style of stone, carvings, and writing. This suggests that they used the same stonemason. Sometimes these can be side by side, so they are easy to distinguish, others are spread across the churchyard. With families using the same stonemasons this allows family historians to find other relatives gravestones. This is especially helpful when they are dedicated to female relatives who may have married and changed their name.

**Women**
Patriarchal authority underlaid all family relationships. Married women could not normally hold property and could not represent themselves in law. A husband was free to administer limited corporal punishment to his wife. In most circumstances, a woman was seen as having no right to disobey her husband.[18] Women, like children, are defined by relationships to others whether it is a daughter, wife, or mother. This can be seen very clearly on the stones of women whether they are on the stones with their husband or on their own and it is the father that she is associated with. This is the woman's identity: she is defined by her father until she is married, and is then defined by her husband. What is also prominent with many of the stones dedicated to women is that the name of the husband or father is more elaborate or larger than their daughter or wife. This happens in all churchyards I have visited, and it shows who is dominant, even on the stone of their wife or daughter.

The language used on the gravestones to depict that a woman was a wife is different to that which we use today. There are sentences we

'Relict' gravestone Holy Trinity, Bilsby, Lincolnshire.

Gravestone of Elizabeth Martin All Saints churchyard Leicester.

would expect to find such as *'beloved wife of'* and *'wife of'* etc, but there are others. The word *'relict'* appears on many gravestones and monuments, both inside and outside of churches. The word means 'widow of a man' and has been used since c.1460.[19] The word spans all the time periods present, but seems to become less frequent into the nineteenth century, and has vanished altogether into the twentieth century. It is a very formal word and reads with no passion or expression of emotions that the husband and the family would have been going through at that time. An example of this is from Holy Trinity churchyard in Bilsby, Lincolnshire.

> *'In memory of Hannah Relict of Anthony Abbott who died at Alford January 10th 1846 aged 88 years'*

The inscription is very formal and lacks emotion; there are no images or passage of text on the stone at all. It seems a very impersonal way to commemorate a wife of a member of the family. It is also found on family stones where both the husband and wife are depicted. There is also no male equivalent word present on any of the stones.

Another word on gravestones that is specific to women is spinster.

*'To the memory of Elizabeth Martin spinster who departed this life 2nd July 1853 in the 56th year of her age.'*

Also inside St Margaret's Church, Leicester:

*'In memory of Mary Lane spinster who died 6th September 1802 aged 51.'*

A spinster was a woman who was not married, and which society deems above marriageable age. Because this was not the way that a woman's life 'should be', it was seen as a derogatory term. The male equivalent of this is bachelor, but this was not, as today, seen as a derogatory term, and I have not come across this being present on the gravestones for men. Unfortunately, the historical records are very limited for these women, and it is the gravestones that give us the most information.

There are sometimes gravestones that comprise purely of the names of women, as can be seen on the gravestone of the Lancaster women in St Mary's churchyard Snettisham.

*Gravestone of the Lancaster women in St Mary's churchyard Snettisham, Norfolk.*

This is the grave of Harriet Lancaster, her sister Martha Lancaster, and their niece Harriot Lancaster. There is no evidence of marriage on the stone for any of these women and no mention of the word spinster either. However, when we delve a little deeper the historical records can shed some light on these women. From the 1901 census, a year before Harriet died, both Harriet aged 74 and Martha 71 were single and living off their own means at The Gables Snettisham, Norfolk, with a cook and a housemaid.[20] How then were these two women able to support themselves? The previous census records can help. Both Harriet and Martha worked as housekeepers, earning their own money. Their probate records show that Harriet and Martha both left large sums of money to their families.

*Sarah Barrows epitaph St Margaret's churchyard Leicester.*

One of the most common forms of death for women during the seventeenth, eighteenth and nineteenth century was death in, or because of, childbirth. This could have been because of birth complications, infection, or medical malpractice. A great deal is known of the rate of infant mortality during this period, and it is evident on the stones in vast numbers, if not in detail. The mention of women dying in childbirth is not mentioned as often as it probably happened, but I have come across a few cases.

In St Margaret's churchyard, Leicester:

> *'Sarah the wife of John Barrow after giving birth to her third child suddenly expired in 1835 aged 28 years. In the same grave 24 days later were deposited the remains of her infant Sarah Wright Barrow.'*

St Mary's Church, Bideford, Devon:

> *'Here Lie the remains of Mary the wife of Richard Eastman who died in childbed with her tenth child 22nd April 1805 aged 41 years.'*

St Mary De Castro, Leicester:

> *'To the memory of Ann wife of Thomas Allsop she died in Child-birth the 11th of April 1779 aged 33 years.'*

> *'Near this place are deposited the earthly remains of Ann Cort wife of James Cort daughter of the Rev Thomas Robinson who at the early age of 29 years having had ten children and leaving five to lement* [sic] *her loss finished her short afflicted cause…* [final lines are submerged]

St Martin's Church, Leicester:

> *'In mournful and most affectionate remembrance of the late Elizabeth Vaughan who died in child-bed January 16th 1808 aged 26.'*

These are loving family stones with sentiments about the loss of a mother and what they have left behind. They give us a sense of the fleeting nature of life, and the risks that women were putting themselves through time and time again.

However, even when death in childbirth is not recorded, the gravestones can hold other clues that it was the cause. This is where the date of the infant dying, if present, was very close to that of the mother, or where the age of the wife is young. Using the age of a woman to determine what she died from is obviously pure speculation, but as society expected marriage and children, any guess would be an educated one.

The historical records that would back this theory up are non-existent as death certificates were not reliable, or perhaps didn't even exist when these women died, so the gravestones are the only evidence that we have for this type of death in this era. However, things were beginning to change. In the report published in 1861 by J.C. Steele *Numerical Analysis of Patients treated at Guys Hospital for the last seven years, from 1854 to 1861,* he lists the number of women who came to the maternity department in the hospital. The total number of women who attended Guys Hospital was 11,928 over the seven years; this seems rather small given the number of women that were most likely having children at the time. This shows that it was most likely the upper and upper-middle classes that were having their confinement in hospital. What is surprising though is the number of women who were in their twelfth confinement – 107 or higher. The report shows that one woman was in her twenty-second. This is an unthinkable number of pregnancies today.

The report also tells us that over 500 babies were stillborn, how many mothers died and the cause of death. Thirty-six women died at the hospital, most from complications with birth. But there are a few other causes such as cholera, pneumonia and fever. Most women, however, would have given birth at home attended by other women and never set foot in a hospital. If they had, from the evidence I have from the gravestones, I can imagine that the numbers would be far higher.

## Wills and Legacy

Today the writing of wills and stating what you are going to leave to which family members is very common, but it is usually a private affair done behind closed doors with a solicitor –not something you would find written on a gravestone. However, many churches and churchyards have stones and monuments that state exactly what people have done and left for their families. From the thirteenth to the eighteenth century the will was a means by which a person could express, very often in a personal manner, his religious faith, his attachment to his possessions, to the beings he loved, and to God, and to the decisions he had made to ensure his salvation.[21]

The Principal Probate Registry was established on 12 January 1858 and keeps a copy of every will proved in England and Wales after 1858.[22] These can be searched though the national archives website and through ancestry.com and findmypast.co.uk. Not everyone made a will however, perhaps because they had nothing to leave, or it was a small amount and was sorted out through family and friends. Before 1858 if a will was made and needed to be administered by executors then it had to go to probate court, which was usually a church court. Wives needed permission from their husbands to make and leave a will so most female testators were widows or spinsters.[23]

The writing of the deceased's legacy on a stone or memorial was a way to ensure that their family or the parish did not forget them, what they had done, or wanted to do. It can also give valuable information to family historians and genealogists, especially if it is the only written evidence of what they left.

In the churchyard at St Mary de Castro Leicester, is the stone of Thomas Clarke who was a servant in the house of John Pares Esq. for forty-five years and his stone tells us:

*'Beneath are deposited the remains of Thomas Clarke for five and forty years a faithful servant and honoured inmate in the life of John Pares Esq. He departed this life October 3rd 1823 at the advanced age of 88*

*and bequeathed among his surviving relatives rewards of two thousand pounds the honest earnings of his long and faithful service.'*

That is a vast amount of money for anyone to leave a family in the 1800s, and because this was left on his gravestone I went in search of his will. Thomas left a detailed will of how his £2,000 should be split across his family. From this it tells us that he was not married and that his executor was the son of his master, Thomas Pares Esq. There are also little details in it that are very helpful to the family historian, it states that he was a yeoman and living in Groby at the time of writing his will. It also lists many different and indirect relations to whom he left money, and what their relationship to him was. He left sums of money to nieces, nephews and children of deceased half-relatives, which is invaluable information.[24] It is possible that he wanted to show how much his family meant to him and how much he was leaving them. Another possibility is that because his master's family erected the stone, they wanted to show how much he was leaving his family, so others knew how generous they were as an employer.

Inside St Mary De Castro Church there is a memorial on the wall near the door which is dedicated to the whole Palmer family. The stone was erected by the will of daughter Jane Palmer. It is a large elaborate monument and gives very complimentary statements about Jane Palmer who 'in her last will and testament did enjoy this small monument to be erected'. It states that she did this for the memory of her parents. This in turn ensures that they too are remembered, it gives the whole family an identity and shows that Jane Palmer wanted to make sure that the monument was erected.

The tomb of Gabriel Newton in All Saints' churchyard Leicester, is very grand and has his life's work written around the edge. He was a high-ranking official and benefactor for education in Leicester and had written on his tomb his 'last will directed 3250 pounds to be raised out of his personal estate for supporting a charity of kind in Leicester'.

Also inside All Saints' Church is the wall monument of Elizabeth Charlotte Mason who died 13 December 1833 aged 58 years and the plaque states:

*'In the year 1832 she built and by her will endowed four houses in the parish for the reception of poor aged females of the town of Leicester.'*

Elizabeth was of middle- to upper-class standing. There is no husband stated and she left her own will, but as if that wasn't enough, in her will she is described as 'a spinster'. Otherwise, her money and property would have passed to her husband. All Saints' parish church is situated on the outskirts of Leicester, and at that time her bequest would have been very much needed. The four houses were in Vauxhall Street, and in her will she left the residue of her property, amounting to £1,420, for the endowment of the alms houses; the interest of which provided the four almswomen four shillings a week.[25]

All the stones that are mentioned state what they have left or done for their family or the community. But wills were also used in other ways – to tell families exactly how a person wanted to be buried. Clare Gittings, a researcher from the National Portrait Gallery in London, investigated twenty-six individual burials where the deceased had stated in their wills exactly what was to happen at their funeral and how they wanted to be buried. Many of those she researched were very unusual, such as a ceremony and burial in a cave, the body to be dissected and only the bones deposited in the grave.[26] This demonstrates how a person's identity can be vividly expressed in their will. In 1869, Charles Dickens wrote in his will that he wanted a 'private' and 'unostentatious' funeral when he died.[27]

Family and identity go hand in hand, it is what defines us. It is where we come from and who we are. It is very clear to see from the gravestones and memorials inside and outside of the church that family is the most common theme of identity and some of the most valuable information that we can gain. Nearly all the stones are associated with a relative even if, as with a child, they are not named specifically, they still have the identity through the family.

*Chapter 3*

# OCCUPATIONS

What someone does for a living has been a defining part of a person's identity. Even today, when meeting people for the first time, one of the first questions that we ask to find out about the person is what they do for a job. It is the same with researching our family history; we want to know what our ancestors did. Their occupation defined their status, how they were seen in society and how they wanted to be remembered.

During the medieval period it was common for people to have a by-name describing their craft or trade. The occupational by-names were used to distinguish people from others who had the same name.[1] The poll tax records of the fourteenth century can shed a light on the occupations that were around through that period from the study of the surnames present. This can also be very true with gravestones; however, it is in a more direct fashion.

Gravestones can show a great variety of occupations, some that we would recognise today, others that we no longer have or require. This is not, however, through a person's surname. The occupations of many have been written on the stones directly, and not just on their own but on their family's stones too. The occupation of a person is what they may have had from a very young age. They were possibly apprenticed and then progressed through a trade; it may have been a family-run business, or perhaps they followed in the footsteps of their father. It may have taken a lot of money and time to train and gain the experience to enter certain occupational fields. There are many types of occupations that appear, so I have split them into the following categories, political, general, religious, and the occupations of women. I will look at each of these occupational fields and explore what jobs are present on the stones and explain a bit about them.

## Political occupations

During the eighteenth, nineteenth and the vast majority of the twentieth century, the way that a city and borough was run was very different to what we have today. Before 1835 the governing body of a place, which was called a corporation, consisted of the mayor, twenty-four aldermen (including the mayor), and forty-eight common councilmen. The mayor elected the aldermen from the common councilmen, and this was a position held for life; the councilmen were elected out of the freemen of the borough. The aldermen also elected the offices of the corporation.[2] Below is a list of the political offices that are present on the gravestones and memorials.

| Political occupations |
|---|
| Alderman |
| Mayor |
| Justice of the peace |
| Recorder |
| High sheriff |
| Chief Magistrate |
| Supervisor of excise |
| Macebearer |
| Town clerk |
| Clerk of the Parish |

*List of the political occupations.*

Most of these are found in cities rather than the rural churchyards. Alderman is the most common position mentioned. It is not surprising that the richest parishes had the highest number of aldermen. As mentioned above the role of the alderman is for life and it was a senior member of the county or city councils' administration and had legislative, judicial, and administrative functions. However, the role of mayor was not. It is clear from the epitaphs on gravestones that mayoralty was held for one year, but a mayor could be elected more than once. From St Margaret's churchyard Leicester, is the stone of Joseph Burbidge who was, 'one of the aldermen of the borough and served as mayor in the year 1792'.

I have found three memorials that give the year that they were mayor: Joseph Burbidge 1792, James Bishop 1782, and William Bellamy 1799, all from St Margaret's churchyard Leicester. Most of the stones and memorials read 'once mayor' or 'twice mayor'.

The other positions only appear on a very few of the memorials and are important job roles during that time. The role of the Recorder was established by Letters Patent in 1464 and the Recorder was a judicial officer who applied himself to reading the records of the town and was legal head of the Borough Quarter Sessions until the office was abolished in 1971. He was required to visit the borough at least four times a year to preside over the Borough Quarter Sessions, where local people stood trial for criminal offences.[3] Justice of the Peace (JP) was an inferior magistrate appointed to preserve the peace in a county, town, or other district. The JP's principal duties consist of committing offenders to trial before a judge and jury when satisfied that there is a *prima facie* case against them, convicting and punishing summarily in minor causes, and granting licenses.[4] This job appears on many gravestones however it is written in different ways. Sometimes the job is written in full text and includes other parts of the job that he did making it obvious what his job was.

St Martin's Church Leicester:

> 'To the memory of John Simpson Esq late one of His Majesty's Justices of the Peace and Receiver General of the land tax for this county who died November 29 1758 aged 60.'

In other instances, it just uses the abbreviations 'JP', which was the well-known abbreviation for that occupation at the time, this can also be seen in the historical directories and in the newspapers over the times:

> 'In affectionate memory of John Heath Williams JP who departed this life June 6 1899.'

The role of JP was instituted in England in 1327.[5] The memorial to John Whatton in St Martin's Church Leicester is the earliest I have found so far with the occupation mentioned. He died in 1656 and was 'Justice of the Peace for the county of Leistr' under King Charles', and this is stated on his memorial.

The Chief Magistrate held exclusive jurisdiction for the Borough and concurrent jurisdiction with the county magistrates and presided over the serious criminal cases.[6] The Supervisor of Excise or Officer of Excise is today what we would know today as a tax collector, they collected taxes on household products such as alcohol, tobacco, and betting licences.

In St Margaret's churchyard is the gravestone to two men who were both Officers of Excise:

> 'In memory of Richard Peacock a native of Bulmer in Yorkshire and late officer of excise in this town he died 28th oct 1831 aged 35 years Also John Robinson late officer for excise who died 21st march 1827 aged 40 years.'

Why these two men were commemorated together is not known; it is possible that they had known each other through their line of work, but the records do not show any other contact or that they were related. So far, I have not been able to find any evidence that either man married. This occupation was often seen as unpopular and both men would have been known by many traders in the town. It is possible that their burial, and stone was provided by the corporation or a charity.

St Martin's churchyard also has a gravestone that mentions the Officer for Excise.

> 'Sacred to the memory of Robert Lister Officer for Excise in the Parish who departed this life 4th March 1798 aged 53 years.'

This grave is earlier that the previous two and we know that he was married as his wife Ann is buried with him, and that the gravestone was erected by his daughters as this is stated on the stone, although very hard to read.

The occupation of Town Clerk was conferred upon a professional lawyer and was appointed by the aldermen of the corporation.[7] These two occupations can be seen side by side in St Martin's Church on the memorials to Thomas Heyrick 'an attorney at law and served the office of Town Clerk from 1745 to 1764', and also John Heryick, 'an eminent solicitor and Town Clerk of this Borough 26 years'. They very often practised law alongside being the clerk for the town. The office of High Sheriff is an ancient office and Leicester is one of the few towns retaining that title. It was previously called High Bailiff but the modern name of Sheriff took its place.[8]

The office that we do not have today is that of Macebearer. There is only one stone that mentions this job and it is situated against the wall near the entrance to St Martin's Church Leicester and the entrance to the Guildhall Museum opposite.

The stone reads:

> 'Sacred to the memory of Joseph Smith who departed this life 16th January 1826 aged 77 years. He Held the office of Macebearer for this borough and during a period of twenty five years discharged the duties of that office with zeal and fidelity.'

*Gravestone of Joseph Smith Macebearer St Martin's churchyard Leicester.*

The role of the macebearer was to parade the mace on civic occasions and when the corporation required it. The top of the stone has the Leicester municipal Cinquefoil emblem, which is still the emblem for Leicester city council today. The emblem and the inscription show that he wanted to be remembered for his time as Macebearer. This is a very poignant stone, as Joseph Smith was one of the last holders of the ancient office of Macebearer.[9]

The office of Macebearer disappeared after the introduction of the Municipal Corporation Act 1835.[10] The act was brought in after a royal commission was appointed to investigate the corporations in England and Wales.[11] The existing corporation for Leicester was replaced with elected officials from each of the wards. This was done by the rate-paying households of the borough, who had resided in the borough for more than three years. Previously the old corporation vacancies had been filled by co-optation.[12] One of the main things that happened was that the new council got rid of much of the town's pageantry, which included the role of Macebearer. The Great Mace, together with the town's plate, was sold off.[13] Mrs Laughton of Wharf Street bought the Great Mace at auction for £85. The Mace was finally returned to the corporation in 1866 and was only to be used on proper civic occasions.[14]

The Municipal Corporation Act of 1835 changed the way that the whole corporation worked and was run. Aldermen no longer held the position for life, but for only six years with half of the aldermen going out of office every third year. The mayor was also elected annually and people who were duly qualified for the roles were chosen, rather than being selected based on their family ties and acquaintances.[15] None of the aldermen and mayors that are mentioned on the stones served office after the Act was introduced so many of their predecessors are most likely buried in cemeteries across the city.

## General Occupations

The general occupations that are mentioned on the stones and memorials are varied and the table below shows the types of jobs there are. Most are ones we would recognise today as they still exist in some form. I won't discuss all those listed as not all of them were legible enough to get information, or there wasn't any more information to find.

| Occupations | | | |
|---|---|---|---|
| Surgeon | Liquor merchant | Ship Builder | School Master |
| Doctor (MD) | Keeper of the County Gaol | Hatter | Stud Groom |
| Solicitor | Keeper of Mitre and Keys | Servant | Printer |
| Architect | Keeper of the House of Correction | Housekeeper | Butcher |
| Coroner | Governor of the workhouse | Stationer | Farm Bailiff |
| Goldsmith | Hosier | Carpenter | Bailiff |
| Grocer | Frame smith | Midwife | Colliery worker |
| Ironmonger | Musician | Druggist | Quarryman |
| Librarian | Secretary to newsroom | Stagecoach man | Gamekeeper |
| Master Mariner | Merchant | Seaman/Mariner | |

The occupations of surgeon, doctor and coroner are the same occupations in title that we know today. But in practice, during the eighteenth and nineteenth centuries they would have been very different. Not all surgeons or doctors were qualified or had received training, and those that had usually charged, so were accessible only to those who could afford it.

There have been several instances where the memorial has mentioned the occupation of surgeon or doctor. Inside Holy Trinity Church Tattershall, Lincolnshire, is the memorial of John Marston Surgeon:

> 'Near the north door are interred the remains of John Marston Surgeon for nearly thirty years an active and skilled practitioner at Tattershall in the county died Decr 30th 1839 aged 59.'

This is a very complementary memorial to John Marston and suggests that he was well respected and a good surgeon.

In St Wilfrid's churchyard Alford, Lincolnshire:

> 'In memory of John Hannah Surgeon who departed this life April 26th 1832 aged 32 years.'

This memorial is the largest in the churchyard and stands at the front of the church for all to see. John Hannah is listed as one of three surgeons in Alford in 1826 *Whites Directory* in the Butter Market and in *Pigots Directory* for Alford in 1829.

It took a lot of work, time and money to become qualified in these occupations and involved attending university. We know this from the memorial of George Shaw from Saint Martin's Church Leicester that reads.

> 'Also of George Shaw Doctor of Medicine of the University of Cambridge born Halifax Yorkshire November 7 1801 died at Leicester November 10 1888.'

This is a rather special monument as at the time of George's death in 1888 the government had passed a number of Burial Acts which prohibited burials in churches; the Home Secretary at the time granted special permission for George to be buried in the vault with his wife who had died forty-three years previously.[16] The information that this monument gives, and the year in which he died, has given me the opportunity to delve deeper into George Shaw's life. As his monument states, he attended the University of Cambridge. This was a very prestigious university in the nineteenth century, as it is today, and it would have taken a lot of work and wealth to gain entry. With this information I was able to trace him in the Cambridge University Alumni documents. This record tells us that George was admitted to Caius college on 3 March 1818, and his formal admission as a student was at Michaelmas 1819. The document also records some of his achievements in his field. He was a Fellow of the Royal College of Physicians, a senior physician at the Leicester Royal Infirmary and a Justice of the Peace for Leicester.[17] This information is also backed up by census records, all of which between 1851 and 1871 state that he was a physician and a Fellow of the Royal College of Physicians. In the 1881 census he is 79 and still a physician, but it also tells us that he was a Justice of the Peace for this year. We know that George was successful and wealthy. Throughout this period, he was living at 16 New Street, which is near St Martin's Church in the centre of the city of Leicester and that he had a housekeeper, servants and a footman. We know the extent of this wealth from his probate entry, which states that his estate was £28,063 16s 6d. He also left his home 16 New Street to his housekeeper, Eliza Flude.[18]

### 1889.

SHAW George M.D.
Personal Estate £28,063 16s. 6d.

5 January. The Will of George Shaw late of Leicester in the County of Leicester M.D. who died 10 November 1888 at Leicester was proved at Leicester by Eliza Flude of New-street Leicester Spinster John Sarson of Kibworth Harcourt in the said County Gentleman and the Reverend James Armitage Bonser of Shillington in the County of Bedford Clerk Vicar of Shillington the Executors.

SHAW—November 10, at 16, New Street, Leicester, George Shaw, M.D. Cantab., F.R.C.P.L., Justice of the Peace for the county and borough of Leicester, in the 88th year of his age.

*Probate Register for George Shaw www.ancestry.co.uk and Death Notice, The Belfast Newsletter November 15th, 1888, www.ancestry.co.uk.*

This gravestone and the information it represents is a bit of an enigma; if the Home Secretary of the time had not granted permission for George to be buried with his wife, would we have the information on him? He had no children to oversee the burial, would he have been buried in one of the new cemeteries on the city limits and would the information regarding his birth, death and career have been recorded?

The memorial for Edward Entwhistle Wilkinson, also from inside Saint Martin's Church, states that he was also a surgeon:

*'In affectionate remembrance of Edward Entwhistle Wilkinson esq nearly twenty years surgeon at the Leicester Royal Infirmary who died 4th July 1846 aged 50 years.'*

From newspapers at the time, we know that Edward Wilkinson was part of the committee of Governors of the Infirmary and took on the role of Temporary Secretary in 1823.[19]

The other stones I have found that state the occupation of surgeon or doctor just mention the word 'surgeon', 'doctor', and 'coroner', with no other information at all. However, these can also be enlightening too. In the churchyard of Holy Trinity Bilsby is the grave of Mary Jean Jacobsen.

*'In loving memory of Mary Jean beloved wife of G. Oscar Jacobsen for some time surgeon at Alford who departed this life 5th March 1916 aged 50.'*

When I saw this, I went hunting for the grave of her husband G. Oscar Jacobsen and I could find none. With the gravestone telling us that he was a surgeon and where, and details of his wife, I was able to dig a bit deeper and find Dr Jacobsen on the medical register of 1913 which shows us that he became a member of the Royal College of Physicians and the Royal College of Surgeons in 1889, and that he was living on West Street in Alford.[20] After which the trail goes cold but I did find him on a passenger list to New Zealand a few months after the death of Mary Jean in 1916.[21] The mention of Dr Jacobsen on the grave of his wife opened up a whole new line of enquiry which otherwise we may not have known.

The Keeper of the House of Correction and Keeper of the County Gaol are intriguing and terrifying occupations in the same measure. They are very similar jobs in that they involve looking after inmates in the gaol and house of correction. There is only one mention in the churchyards and churches of each of these occupations and they are both found in St Mary de Castro's churchyard Leicester:

*'In memory of James Staples Late Keeper of the Gaol of the county of Leicester who departed this life on the 15th April 1811 aged 37 leaving a widow and seven infant daughters.'*

*'In memory of William Phillips Late Keeper of the House of Correction for this county January 29th 1821 age 74 years.'*

Leicester's first County Gaol was completed in 1309 and sited on the High Street, which is now Highcross Street. The gaol was then moved to the corner of Highcross Street and Free School Lane in 1790–92.[22] The reason for the movement of the gaol was that it was in such an appalling state and John Howard, a prison reformer of the time, condemned it.[23] In his report John Howard described the horrible conditions and the circumstances in which the prisoners were kept, some with no water, food or fresh air, and 'gaol fever' killed more than the executions did. He proposed many reforms.[24] It was very hard sometimes to tell the difference between the prisoners and the gaolers. It was only the presence of the gaoler's irons, handcuffs and keys that separated them from the prisoners.[25] This was not just in Leicester, it was the same for gaols up and down the country.

The Houses of Correction, or Bridewells, were an adaptation of the 1601 Elizabethan poor law.[26] It was a place where work could be forced upon the idle and the vagabonds who refused to do it. However, they were not part of the poor relief system, as that dealt with the settled poor (people who found themselves temporarily out of work, who were born in the parish, or had married into it). The Houses of Correction were for the wandering poor and for people who were unable to support themselves.[27] Over time the Houses of Correction were used for the punishment and reform of petty criminals by subjecting them to short terms of imprisonment and hard labour. The Justices of the Peace preferred to send people to the Houses of Correction as a trial was not needed. The original House of Correction in Leicester was situated on Blue Boar Lane and was moved to the rear of the County Gaol in 1804. It was at this prison that James Staples and William Phillips worked. Unfortunately, these buildings no longer exist. After the building of the new gaol on Welford Road, which opened in 1828 and is still the city's prison today, the original gaol and House of Correction were sold.[28]

The workhouse is an institution that we have all heard of, but thankfully will never experience. Unfortunately this was not the case for our predecessors. The grave of William Flint stands in the churchyard of St Margaret's church Leicester, the parish in which he was the workhouse governor. The workhouse was built in 1714 and stood near the present Vestry Street, in Humberstone Gate.

> *'Sacred to the memory of William Flint late governor of Saint Margaret's Workhouse who died November 19 1833 aged 53 years.'*

Under the old Poor law i.e., before the Poor Law Act of 1834, each parish across the country was responsible for its own care of the poor. Indoor and outdoor poor relief was supposed to be for the 'settled poor' of the parish, and the levying of a poor rate raised the money for this from the middle and upper classes.[29] This led to many discrepancies across the country as to what relief was given and how it was given. This led to some people being denied poor relief and being turned away to other parishes, sometimes with no good reason. We have evidence that William Flint did just that from a newspaper article in the *Leicester Journal* of 4 January 1833: at the quarter sessions, William Flint and various others were found to have sent a married couple to the village of Great Glenn, a parish in the county of Leicestershire, without any warrant or authority.

> ST. MARGARET'S PARISH.—At the County Quarter Sessions, held yesterday at the Castle, a True Bill was found against William Thornton, Acting Overseer: Thomas Pickering, Vestry Clerk; William Flint, Workhouse Master, and George Banks, constable, for a *Conspiracy* against the parish of Great Glenn, in this county, for conveying Peter Canning and Mary his wife, casual poor, from the parish of St. Margaret to the parish of Great Glenn, without any warrant or authority whatever.

Leicester Journal, *William Flint article 4th January 1833, British Newspaper Archive.*

It is important to note the lack of low status occupations that occur on the stones. As can be seen in the table, most occupations are grand and high status, or are jobs that people valued and wanted to be remembered by. What is quite remarkable for Leicester especially is that there is only mention of one 'hosier' and one 'frame smith'. These memorials both occur inside churches, one inside St Mary de Castro and one inside St Margaret's. The hosiery trade before the mid-eighteenth century was almost alone in the major employment of the time. No other industry came close to offering work on the same scale.[30] During the nineteenth century it was still a dominant industry. The principal article of manufacture was that of the stocking, and in 1822 on average '18,000 dozen per week of stockings are made'.[31] The trade directories of 1822 and 1828 list over 100 manufacturers of hosiery in Leicester. Vast numbers of people worked in the hosiery industry of Leicester; the industry was first established without power-driven machinery and for a very long-time production was not confined to a crowded factory.[32] In 1833 there were said to be

28,000 persons, including many children, employed in this industry in Leicester, which had a population of nearly 40,000 in 1831.[33] Many of the aldermen and mayors of the town started their careers in the hosiery industry and progressed through. It is surprising with that number of people working in the industry, how very few in the early years have chosen to say that they worked in the industry. It appears that they wanted to be remembered for their political achievements rather than their origins in the town. So, when looking around at gravestones it is always worth remembering to also note what is missing, as this too can give a sense of the people buried there.

In Leicester, this is in direct contrast to other areas of the country where the dominant occupation of all classes of people is there for all to see. This can be seen especially in the churchyards around our coastline. The churchyard of St Mary's Appledore, Devon, has an overwhelming number of monuments dedicated to those who had occupations to do with the sea:

> 'In loving memory of Robert Blackmore shipbuilder who died January 15th 1894 aged 54 years.'
>
> 'In loving memory Philip White Master Mariner who died January 28th 1894 aged 55 years.'
>
> 'In loving memory of James Allport Guard Master Mariner who died January 11th 1890 aged 58.'

*Allport Guard Master Mariner certificate, www.ancestry.co.uk.*

*Gravestones with anchors and ships from St Mary's Appledore, Devon.*

Master Mariner is the most common occupation stated here. A Master Mariner was a licensed mariner who holds the highest grade of seafaring qualification and is issued with a certificate to prove this. They would serve as the head of a merchant ship of any size and type.[34]

One of the most striking things about St Mary's churchyard is that even if you do not read the stones, you would know that the people had an association with the sea, such as shipbuilders and sailors, because the stones had it carved into them with the presence of many and often large carvings of anchors and ships.

It was not just the sea that monopolised whole populations of people, the coal mining industry did as well. This is the case for my ancestors and has been shown in many areas of Northumberland. It is no coincidence that places are called coal mining towns as many were created for that specific purpose. The mine owners would build houses for their workers so that they could live near the mine where they worked. As a result, it is also where they died. The mining industry in the country has now all but disappeared, and in many areas the people who would remember the mining communities are getting fewer and fewer each year. Again, this is where the churchyards can help. After 1851 the census records can give us a sense of the occupations of a household, a street and whole areas if they survive and are legible. If not, the gravestones can give us the clues.

In the churchyards of Holy Trinity Church Seghill, Northumberland, and St Mary's Horton, Northumberland, we get a glimpse into the lives of the community that worked in the mines.

The following are from Holy Trinity churchyard:

*'In Loving & Affectionate Remembrance of JOHN TAYLOT COATES, the dearly beloved husband of ANNIE COATES & only son of TAYLOR & MARGARET COATES of Annitsford, who lost his life at Seghill Colliery, April 1st 1897, aged 32 years & 10 months.'*

*'THE FAMILY BURIAL PLACE OF JAMES AND ANN FRYAR, of Seaton Delaval Colliery. MARK their son died September 19 1869 Aged 34 Years. ANN the above died Jan 31 1872 aged 65 years. MARK HENDERSON FRYAR, grandson of the above died April 6th 1873 aged 6 years.'*

*'In Affectionate Remembrance of JOHN the beloved husband of ELLEN S. FISHER, who met his death by the Breaking of a Rope at Seaton Delaval Pit, August 19th 1883, aged 30 years.'*

All the graves that are mentioned above came from coal mining families which is shown in the census records by occupations listed. Also, by the names of the roads that they lived on as most of them had a name associated with the mines for example Foreman's Row.

These are just a fraction of the graves that mention the collieries and tragically, most mention an accident of some sort. This topic and more of the graves of St Mary's churchyard Horton are discussed in greater detail in Chapter 5.

## Religious Occupations

As you would expect, there are many religious occupations that are mentioned both inside and outside of the churches. Nearly all the occupations I have come across are still relevant today, so I am not going to focus to heavily on this area as information is widely available on the specifics of these roles. The main ones are those of vicars and reverends of the churches, and one of the most useful things about these is that they can list the places that they have held service over the years and how long for, which can be very helpful to track the movements of your ancestors through the records, as clergy tended to go where the church told them to go. Even the most remote churches have dedications to people associated with the church. St Michael's Church, which is situated on the granite top of Brentor on Dartmoor, has a grave dedicated to a descendant of the founder of the church. There are also stones that say what that person did in the parish or for the church, such as sexton, churchwarden, bell ringer and choirmaster. Holding these offices meant something to those who were leaving them, and it is the identity they want to share with the people who still visit the church, especially if the memorial is inside the church. Having a family member with a religious occupation can be very helpful, especially if researching women as shown in Chapter 2 on family; female ancestors are associated with the males in their family and if their husband or father held a religious occupation, especially a high ranking one then they are often allowed to be buried inside the church allowing for their details to survive. An example of this is from St Mary's Church Snettisham, Norfolk, with the wall memorial to Lucy Herring. This memorial is doubly special because it also tells us that it as been restored after being bombed in 1916. I wonder what information that we have lost to memorials that have never been restored and are now lost.

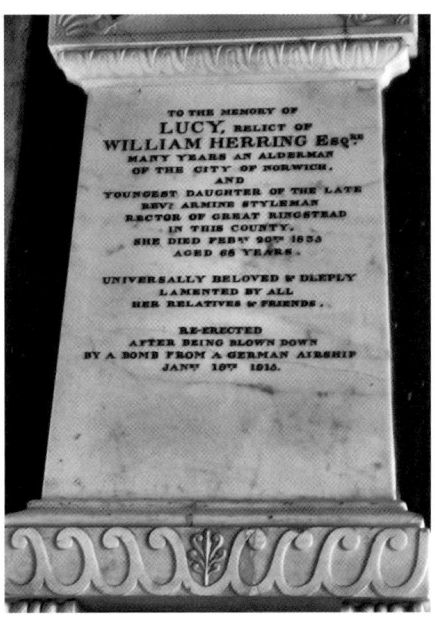

*Wall memorial to Lucy Herring St Mary's church Snettisham, Norfolk.*

## Occupations of Women

The occupations of women are not widely seen on gravestones, especially if they were married. Women were expected to look after their husbands, their children and home, even if they did have jobs to supplement the household income the family and the home came first. However, in All Saints' churchyard Loughborough, Leicestershire, I came across the (now lying flat) gravestone of Catherine Forman.

> 'In remembrance of Cath;n Foreman midwife late wife of Joseph Foreman who departed this life on the 12th December 1816 aged 56 years.'

This is all written on the righthand side of the gravestone with the left side blank, presumably for Joseph her husband. It states that Catherine was a midwife. She would have been practising this trade in the 1700s, and during this period there was no formal training of midwives. Catherine would have learnt her trade by watching other midwives/wise women, most likely in her family and her community. The historical records for women are few and far between for this period. However, I have discovered that Catherine went over to America as there is a newspaper extract from the *Columbian Centinel* 22 March 1817 which details Catherine's death in Loughborough, it also states the number of midwifery cases she was involved with, which is in the thousands.[35] This is not surprising however, as we have seen in previous chapters the number of children that women were having.

The other occupations that have been directly linked to women on the gravestones are those of housekeepers and servants.

In St Peter's churchyard Belgrave, Leicester:

> 'Erected as tribute of affection to the memory of Mary Beeby for many years Housekeeper to Mr Joseph Goddard of Leicester who died February 20th 1834 aged 61 years.'

> 'Erected in memory of Dorothy Groocock (many years housekeeper) to the late Willm Bradley Gent who died 5th March 1856 in the 33rd year of her age.'

St Mary De Castro churchyard Leicester:

> 'In affectionate remembrance of Sarah Sletcher a humble follower of the beloved Jesus she lived fifty six years as Housekeeper in Mr Webb's family in the Market Place in this town respected and beloved and died deeply

regretted November 24 1831 aged 78 years. A member of Mr Webb's family has erected this tribute to her memory to record the long and faithful service of one of the best and most excellent of women.'

Inside the church of St Mary De Castro:

'Near this spot are interred the remains of Ann Grocock for forty-eight years a faithful servant in the family of John Stockdale Esq of this parish she departed this life on the 22nd September 1820 aged 75 years as a slight acknowledgement of numerous kindnesses and attentions received from her in his childhood this memorial is placed by John Stockdale Hardy.'

At the bottom of the Attens family monument:

'… And Sarah Atkins a faithful servant of the family for 34 years died January 13th 1839 aged 54 years.'

Holy Trinity churchyard Bilsby, Lincolnshire:

'In affectionate remembrance of Mary Portas, who died at Alford, October 6th 1869, Aged 84 Years. A faithful and devotedly attached servant and friend to three generations of the family of Sibthorp Canwick Hall Lincoln.'

The role of the housekeeper was of great importance to the household. If the male head of a house was widowed or single, then the duties of the housekeeper would be like that of a housewife. She would be there to cook, clean and look after the children if there was no nanny in the house. A housekeeper was always addressed as Mrs out of respect for her position, even though most of the time they were unmarried. As a housekeeper the women were to be of exceptional character and have a vast array of skills as we can see from newspaper advertisements requiring new housekeepers.

> **HOUSEKEEPER WANTED.**
> WANTED, in a Large Establishment,— A HOUSEKEEPER, who thoroughly understands her business. She must have at least three years' good character from her last place.—Address to A. Z., Post-office, Romsey, stating age, qualifications, and wages required, and giving references as to character. [9667

*Housekeeper advert* Salisbury and Winchester Journal *3rd June 1865, British Newspaper Archive.*

> **HOUSEKEEPER WANTED**
>
> TO Keep the House of a single Gentleman where no Under-servant is ordinarily engaged. A middle-aged Woman would be preferred, who must be able to give undeniable Reference as to Character, Capability, &c.
>
> Apply to Mr. Scott, Publisher of this Paper. If by Letter, Post-paid.

*Housekeeper advert* Carlise Patriot *31st January 1829, British Newspaper Archive.*

What is very clear from the gravestones is that these women stayed with the same family for a long time. They had a secure safe job with a roof over their head and food. For an unmarried female especially, this would not necessarily have been easy to come by. These women made a lasting impression on the families that they worked for, and it was because of this that they left the memorials to honour them.

The occupation that is chosen in life can have a profound effect on the identity of that person, whether it is through your name that it defines you, or it is carved in stone for all to see. If it is carved on the stones, then it is something for which you want to be remembered; it is who you are and what you did. It can be your achievements as a political leader, part of a family tradition or areas work, or saving lives as a doctor; it is part of your identity.

*Chapter 4*

# MILITARY GRAVESTONES AND COMMEMORATIONS

War and combat. This is probably one of the most frequently recognised way that a person has died. Every parish church, cemetery, village, town and city has a war memorial that details the names of men and women who were lost during the two world wars and beyond. When writing this, deciding how and where to incorporate the military gravestones was a dilemma. They hold such a vast amount of information with the details they give us of how and where the men died, the family they are with, the place they are interred, what they achieved in the military as a career, and the style and imagery they used. They are also one of the most emotive types of stones to investigate. The subject of many of these stones cross over into several chapters, so I decided to give them their own, where I will be able to discuss and research them to try and tell a little of their stories. I am going to look at both personal graves set up by the families, and Commonwealth War Graves; at the graves of those who want to be remembered for their military achievements in life, who chose it for a career but who did not fall in combat, and then those who died in combat.

Military commemoration is apart from 'normal' commemoration. Very often the person has died at a young age, often suddenly, and often away from home. Private gravestones of military personnel have a great variety of forms and, not unexpectedly, follow the fashions of the day. Military gravestones in parish churchyards are often not located in separate areas from others but are on or alongside family graves or those of similar date. They offer a glimpse into some of the most turbulent and horrific periods of history where the historical records are lacking due to haste, destruction and loss.

## Before the Great War

Britain has always been, and still is, a military nation. We would not have had the British Empire without the military. This fact is highlighted very well on the graves of men who served. There is, however, no real uniformity with the pre-world-war graves. They are personal to the families and the individuals that they are commemorating. There are also several graves that commemorate the person with their military career who did not fall in battle. A gravestone I found in All Saints' churchyard Rampton, Nottinghamshire, is a great example of this:

> 'Also John Chilton husband of the above who died 3rd March 1868 aged 89 years. He served under the Duke of Wellington through the Peninsular War and Waterloo'

This grave gives us no evidence of his rank or regiment, but the fact that he served and survived until 89 years old which was an achievement in the mid-1800s needed to be remembered. John is commemorated on his wife's grave along with his son. This information does, however, allow us to delve a bit deeper. From the census records of 1851 and 1861 it tells us that John was a labourer and that he was born in Nottinghamshire. His surname was also spelt with an 'e' (Chelton) instead of an 'i'. This, and the confirmation from his gravestone that he served in the military, meant I was able to find him in the Royal Hospital Chelsea Register of Pensioners. He was a private in the First Regiment of Dragoon Guards and was admitted on 11 December 1817 with varicose veins of the leg; his occupation is listed as 'Labourer'.[1]

In St Mary's churchyard Market Harborough is the grave of Henry Dawkins:

> 'Henry Dawkins Late Farrier Major 3rd or Kings own Dragoons He served 41 years having retired resided in Harborough three years six months he departed this life Febry 8th 1818 aged 65 years leaving seven children....'
> Rest is unreadable.

This grave gives us a vast amount of information that we can investigate further. He was a Farrier Major which is the equivalent rank of sergeant and is part of the wider regiment with his unique role of looking after the horses, as the Kings own Dragoons was a mounted cavalry regiment.[2] We are lucky because Henry's pension records survive and from this, we know that his role within the regiment was a blacksmith. He joined the regiment on 12 March 1773 as a private aged 20, and served twenty-five years and fifty-nine days at that rank before being promoted to sergeant, where he stayed for the next eighteen years and ninety-four days until his discharge on 12 August 1814. To ensure that the pension document is presented by the named soldier only, a description is also written on it. Henry was 61 years at date of discharge and was 5 ft 10 in with brown hair and brown eyes. The pension recommendation also mentions his excellent conduct within the regiment.[3] Henry died before census records and without his discharge papers we would not know any of this information, and without his grave stating his career in the military we may never have looked there.

As with today there were many regiments and battalions, some regular and some with specialities. There were also volunteer regiments. The table below shows the different types of military service and the regiments that I have come across split into regular and voluntary units as stated on the graves.

| Regular Units | Voluntary Units |
| --- | --- |
| Royal Navy | Leicestershire Regiment of Militia |
| Royal Marines | Leicester Militia |
| 23rd Royal Welsh Fusiliers | South Devon Militia |
| 1st Regiment of Life Guards | Leicester Volunteer Infantry |
| Leicestershire Yeomanry Cavalry | Leicestershire Volunteers |
| His Majesties 3rd Regiment of Infantry | Leicestershire Yeomanry |
| Royal Regiment of Horseguards | Shropshire Militia |
| Wheatsheaf Division Leicester Corps (St Johns Ambulance) | |
| Leicestershire Regiment | |
| 17th Leicestershire Regiment | |
| 3rd or Kings own Dragoons | |
| Royal Artillery | |
| Northumberland Regiment | |
| Royal Berkshire Regiment | |
| Her Majesties 2nd Regiment of Foot | |

There are many stones and memorials that commemorate men that served in the 'militia'.

St Margaret's churchyard Leicester:

*'Marlborough Yates adjutant of Leicestershire Yeomanry died Nov 20 1799 aged 38 years.'*

In St Mary De Castro churchyard Leicester:

*'Samuel Elson Qr Master in the Leicestershire Militia 1814 71 years.'*

This was a military force raised from the civilian population of a county or region, to supplement a regular army in an emergency. Leicester, along with many other large towns and cities, has been no stranger to the mustering of soldiers for war. Within her borders in the late fifteenth century the fate of the kingdom was decided at Bosworth Field. The first great age of the volunteer, in Leicester along with elsewhere in the country, was in the era of the French Revolution and Napoleon.

All of these were volunteer groups which involved occasional evenings of drills and a summer training camp with parades around the town, which helped with recruitment. Many of these regiments were formed in the 1790s after a General Meeting of the County of Leicestershire. The militia hoped to attract every respectable inhabitant. The officers were of course high status and the memorials that mention a rank are all high ranks and these are the ones that have left this as their identity on the stones. These regiments were used in times of struggle when the country needed more men to fight, such as the Boer War. However, the Yeomanry Cavalry were also used by magistrates and in politics as a way of helping stop disturbances. With the coming of better times and a better police force this need was reduced. They were, however, also involved in politics of the town because, as long as the names of the great landed families of the county were synonymous with those of political masters, the Yeomanry whose ranks always included officers of those families had a political flavour. The volunteer movements were disbanded and returned when there was need. This was especially true with the coming of the two world wars. Today the volunteer units are called the Army Reserve. People who were involved in the militia did not always fight. There is a gravestone in St Margaret's churchyard of George Ransom:

*'George Ranson who was 15 years drummer in the Leicester Militia died 1792.'*

Then as now, there were many different parts to the army and people were proud to serve their country in any way they could, and to be remembered for it.

Most of the stones look no different to those of the deceased's other family members. However, I have come across a few that are very hard to miss. There is a great example of this in the churchyard of Saint Mary

*Gravestone of Lieutenant Edward William Scott of the Royal Navy, St Mary De Castro churchyard Leicester.*

de Castro Leicester. It is the stone of Lieutenant Edward William Scott of the Royal Navy.

> 'Sacred to the memory of Lieut Edward Willm Scott Royal Navy who departed this life 1st day of October 1834 in the 41st year of his age. As a tribute of sincere affection and regard for departed excellence and valour this stone is erected by his afflected relict Mary eldest daughter of the Late Mr Jonathan Hewitt of this place.'

The stone stands out dramatically from the others around it. The top of the stone is dominated by the carved image of a huge, draped urn in the centre, although this is not unusual in itself; on the right, however, there is a navy war vessel, and on the left an anchor and the shield of Britannia. Without reading the epitaph on the stone, it is clear to see that this is a military gravestone and that they want people who look at this stone to know that they served in the Royal Navy. His 'relict' Mary Lee erected the stone. It is very common with military stones that the person or people who erect the stones are mentioned on them to show what the loss of the person means.

The gravestone of Lieutenant Scott is not the only one that states the navy; there is one more in the city of Leicester churchyards. This is surprising, as the most common place to find naval gravestones is in coastal towns. However, although land-locked Leicester may not seem an obvious repository of nautical association, it has played its part. In 1794 the need to find more men for the rapidly expanding navy led to the passing of an Act of Parliament – the Recruiting Acts of 1795 and 1796. The Act of 1795 required every county to provide a certain number of men for the navy and Leicester's quota was 183. In 1796 a similar Act was passed, and this raised men for the army as well as the navy and Leicester was now contributing 237 men. The second stone to mention the navy is that of William Bellamy in St Margaret's churchyard;

> '...and William Bellamy a Lieutenant in the Royal Navy and serving on board His Majesty's Frigate 'Le Babet' when she floundered in the West Indies in the month of March 1801.'

This inscription is written at the bottom of his father's stone. By stating that he was lost at sea it is clear to everyone that he was serving his country and will be missed. It is a way that the family can give him an identity as that is the last thing that they knew about him. This is also very important as little in known about the ship and what happened. We know that *Le Babet* took part in the Anglo-Russian invasion of Holland in 1799 as it was detailed in *The London Gazette* 28 September 1799.[4] However, after this all we know that she set sail for Jamaica and never returned. This is most telling from Lloyds list, which gives weekly shipping news of arrivals and departures and the *Le Babet* is not mentioned after July 1800.[5]

There are also many other graves that give us details of battles and wars that were fought all over the Empire. In St Mary De Castro churchyard Leicester:

> 'William Stevens Esqr Captain of his majesties [sic] third regiment of infantry' 'Disabled by wounds received in the service of his country in the Peninsular.'

William was upper-class and has a large family memorial inside the church. The details that they have left enabled me to find his obituary notice in the *Leicester Journal and Midland Counties General Advertiser* of 21 October 1814, which tell us that it was at the Battle of Albuera where he received five severe wounds; it was the ball in his left arm that baffled the efforts of medical skill and which caused his death.[6] The Peninsular War (1808–1814) was part of the Napoleonic Wars. The Battle of Albuera took place on 16 May 1811, and saw a mixed corps of British, Spanish and Portuguese in conflict with the French Army of the South.

Inside St Martin's Church Leicester:

> 'To the Glory of God and In Memory Of Francis H Cooper of Wheatsheaf Division Leicester Corps Who Died of Disease Contracted Whilst In Attendance On The Sick And Wounded During The South African Campaign 1899–1902 Died July 3rd 1900 Aged 22 Years Erected By The Members Of His Corps.'

This is a fantastic memorial; simple in its design with just the shape of a shield, but it gives us valuable information. At the top of the memorial there is the emblem of the St John Ambulance, of which Francis Cooper was a member. It not only gives us the place that he died and what he died of, it also gives us the campaign in which he served. From these details I have been able to find out through the historical records that he was a Private, service number 348 and 65909, that he died at Bloemfontein and that his effects of £18 14s were left to his father Francis.[7] His death was also recorded in the *Leicester Chronicle* of 14 July 1900, where it states that he died of enteric fever, now known as typhoid, which unfortunately killed more men in the British Army at this time than the fighting did.

What is written on the stones and memorials of those who have fallen during conflicts is usually very complimentary and words such as 'valour' and 'bravery' are used to describe how they served their country. The stones very often state where they died and often how they died.

The stone of Richard Braginton in St Martin's churchyard Leicester is full of information about his career and where he died. What is very interesting about this stone is that he was not from Leicester but a Quarter Master of the South Devon Militia and that he died 'suddenly on his march to Nottingham in the night after retiring to rest in perfect health'. The stone is very flattering about his career and states that he 'served the regiment with unabated zeal and diligence and loyalty to his king'.

The style of this stone is very common to many of the stones and memorials that have commemorated the fallen at war. The theme throughout all of them is to portray the pride that the individuals would have felt in serving their country, and the loss of the families who have erected the stones on their behalf.

## World Wars

These are the most common graves of war that I have come across alongside the war memorials themselves. Many of these are very personal as the families want more than just a name, and state what happened to them. These graves are an invaluable source of information as many records from the First World War have been lost; a phrase I see regularly when researching this period is 'burnt documents', due to their being destroyed during bombing raids in the Second World War. There are two types of grave to be found for the world wars: personal graves commissioned by the families, and those of the Commonwealth War Graves Commission.

The Commonwealth War Graves Commission (CWGC) was set up by Royal Charter in 1917 during the devastation of the First World War. The mission of the CWGC is to ensure those who died in service, or as a result of conflict, are commemorated, so that they, and the human cost of war, are remembered forever. This was the result of the dedication and foresight of Fabian Ware, who was sent to the front in 1914 in a mobile ambulance unit with the Red Cross. He saw the poor state of the resources for the burial and marking of graves and he lobbied higher authorities to turn his unit into a dedicated team for the dead. One of the main things Fabian Ware wanted was equality for all the fallen. Battle took no notice of rank or status and so the CWGC honoured this, something they continue to do.[8] The CWGC stones are distinctive as they are all uniform in size, shape and colour. The stones contain the military details of the fallen, their name, regiment, and service number, and on the top their regiment emblem. If it is known, then also where they died. The relatives are also able to leave a personal inscription under a religious symbol.

The CWGC website, www.cwgc.org, holds the historical records of all the fallen that they have been able to identify, both here and abroad, and it is a fantastic resource. The records hold information on a soldier's name, regiment, date of death and, if known where they died. They also tell us if they have a gravestone, what type, and if the CWGC provided it, or if they are names on a commemorative wall or plaque here or abroad. The commission also traced families of the fallen and the records hold the names and address of those, which are usually the parents. When a grave is erected in a churchyard or cemetery it is recorded in the gravestone register with the details of the fallen, their family, where it is erected and anything else that they were told or were able to find out at the time. This can be invaluable as you will see further in the chapter.

At the time of both world wars legislation restricted the burial of new graves in the parish churchyards, so consequently many of the CWGC in the UK are in the cemeteries of cities and larger towns. However, this did not always apply to rural or small towns. As a result, there are CWGC stones dotted around in many of the rural parish churchyards.

In the churchyard of St Mary's in Mablethorpe, Lincolnshire, there is a total of eleven CWGC gravestones and in St Mary the Virgin churchyard in Heacham, Norfolk, there are thirteen. Out of the churchyards I have visited these two have the highest number of stones. They span both wars and give a good representation of the types of graves and of those commemorated with CWGC stones. The graves from these two churchyards also cover many sections of the military, they include the Army, Royal Navy, Royal Air Force, Home Guard, and ATS. The types of ranks that are present is listed in the table below.

| Rank | Number of Graves | | |
|---|---|---|---|
| Private | 11 | Stoker 1st class | 1 |
| Ordinary Seaman | 1 | 2nd Lieutenant | 2 |
| Sergeant | 3 | | |
| Captain | 1 | | |
| Volunteer | 1 | | |
| Major | 1 | | |
| Corporal | 1 | | |
| Lieutenant | 2 | | |

*Collection of Commonwealth War Graves from St Mary's churchyard Mablethorpe Lincolnshire.*

On the stones from the CWGC there is no difference between the ranks in terms of how they were commemorated. One of the things that makes the CWGC graves different from personal graves is that where possible they include the service number. This can give us a gateway into their military lives and sometimes their personal lives too. I have delved a little deeper into the records and investigated a few of the CWGC stones. As you would expect, I encountered stories of bravery and sacrifice, but also a few stories that I did not expect, as you will see.

I started first with the graves from St Mary's churchyard in Mablethorpe starting with the First World War.

> **167 PRIVATE
> T.G. DENNIS
> LINCOLNSHIRE REGIMENT
> 30th MARCH 1915 AGED 22**

This gravestone does not give us his full name, however, by knowing the regiment and service number as well as his surname I was able to find his British Army Service record. Unfortunately, this was one of the burnt records – although only the corners were damaged and the record was rather more intact than some I have viewed. Thomas Gould Dennis joined up on 17 September 1914 aged 21 at Grimsby. Before the war he was a clerk. He is listed as having a fresh complexion with hazel eyes and brown hair. He was 5ft 9½ inches and weighed 154lbs on joining and had a good physical development. The record also stated that he was inoculated against typhoid in January 1913.[9] This little fact on one of the last few pages of his record is rather important as it shows that lessons had been learnt from the experiences of war; as we have already seen, previously more men had died of typhoid than from the fighting. It also lists his parents, brother and sisters, and his wife as next of kin, all with addresses. This is incredibly useful for family research. Thomas, though, did not die in combat, he died six months after joining up and was still waiting for deployment. He died on 30 March 1915 at Brocklesby Hall Hospital of congestion of the lungs.[10]

> **L. J. BOGG
> ORDINARY SEAMAN. R.N.
> P/JX.296310
> H.M.M.G.B. 13
> 13TH MAY 1942 AGE 19**

Again, his grave only has the man's initials: L.J. Bogg. His name was Leslie John Bogg and his story is one of heroism. Leslie was wounded on active service aboard the Vessel HMMGB 13. He was then transferred to EMS Hospital Union Road Dover Kent where he died.[11] The newspapers at the time reported his death but were not able to give any details. However, on 10 July 1942 it was reported in the Military Notices of the *London Gazette* that Leslie Bogg was Mentioned in Despatches posthumously, this was awarded for actions against the enemy.[12]

This was also reported with more detail in the newspapers. The *Louth Standard* of 1 August 1942 had an article entitled 'Devotion to Duty', this describes in more detail the circumstances surrounding the wounding of Private Boggs, which subsequently led to his death.

It describes how Leslie Bogg kept fighting until he lost consciousness; he had only seen combat for the first time the previous night. The description we get of Private Bogg is that he was well liked by all, that his death had 'cast a gloom over the whole resort', and that he had been in the Navy for only eight months.[13]

There was one CWGC stone that I did not expect to find, that of Irene Prickett. It is in St Mary's churchyard in Mablethorpe. This surprised me because women were not allowed to take up combat roles. So, I couldn't resist looking deeper into this.

*Newspaper article, L Bogg 'Devotion to Duty' Louth Standard 1st August 1942, British Newspaper Archive.*

> ATS
> W143079 CORPORAL
> IRENE MOSS PRICKETT
> AUX. TERRITORIAL SERVICE
> 1ST MARCH 1946

Irene was part of the Auxiliary Territorial Service (ATS); formed in 1938, the ATS was the women's part of the British Army. The ATS was tasked with a range of vital roles that would free up more men to fight. Initially, these roles included cooks, clerks, orderlies and drivers to name a few. But as the demand for men increased, so did the roles that were undertaken by women. By 1943 the ATS women were supporting over a hundred army roles including serving with anti-aircraft units – although they were not allowed to fire the guns.

The original status of the ATS was that of a volunteer unit. However, in 1941 it was granted full military status, which is why Irene has a service number even though she did not see battle. The ATS took on the same rank structure as the army, and women were subject to court martial for certain offences, the same as the men. Irene was stationed at York camp on Women's Services. From newspaper articles I have been able to find out quite a bit about Irene Prickett. In the *Louth Standard* of 28 March 1942, there is a little section on Irene joining the ATS: 'JOINING UP. Today (Friday) Miss Irene Prickett leaves to join the ATS. Miss Prickett for some time has been employed at the local Gas Co. showrooms.'

On 25 April 1942 there was another article in the *Louth Standard* entitled: 'ARE THEY TOUGH?' The brief article gives details of the great lengths Irene went to when granted a short leave from the ATS to get back home to Mablethorpe from Yorkshire when there were no train connections. She started by getting a lift from Yorkshire to Retford in Nottinghamshire, from there she hitch-hiked to Grimsby, after which she got a further life to Louth and then walked the remainder fourteen miles to Mablethorpe.

We also know from the same newspaper on 18 March 1944 that she was listed among other service personnel as back in Mablethorpe on leave. Hopefully this leave was not as eventful as her first one. However, for Miss Irene Prickett there is rather a tragic end to her story. We know from her gravestone that she died on 1 March 1946. The manner of her death we get from the newspapers. On 2 March 1946 the *Daily Mail* has a small article entitled 'ATS GIRL ON DEMOB LEAVE FOUND DEAD.'[14] On 9 March 1946 the *Louth Standard* reported on the coroner's inquest into Irene's death. The inquest was held by the Louth and District Coroner, Capt. R.H. Helmer MC at Mablethorpe Police Court. The doctor had said that the cause of death was inhaling coal gas carbon monoxide. From the inquest it was revealed that she inflicted the gas from the oven upon herself. It also transpired that Irene was suffering from 'anxiety neurosis' as she had lost her ability to concentrate and had a 'fear of returning to camp'. Evidence from her father was reported and he states that she had spent some time in Shenley Military Hospital before returning home on demobilisation leave. According to the newspaper report, her discharge papers stated

> ARE THEY TOUGH?—A short while ago Miss Irene Prickett joined the A.T.S. and last week-end she was granted a short leave. There were, however, no train connections, and she decided to take a chance in getting through. Her first hop was a lift from somewhere in Yorkshire to Retford. From here she hitch-hiked to Grimsby, after which she got a further lift to Louth, arriving there after the last trains and 'buses had gone. Carrying two cases she set off to walk to Mablethorpe, a distance of 14 miles and landed here at 6 o'clock the following morning.

*Newspaper article, I Prickett 'Are They Tough'* Louth Standard *25th April 1942, British Newspaper Archive.*

she had ceased to fulfil the ATS physical requirements and that she had been notified by the Ministry of Pensions that no pension had been granted. This is one of the reasons, it was reported, that she did not want to carry on as she didn't want to be a burden to her father.[15]

This shows the dramatic affect that war can have even if you are not in the midst of battle.

> MAJOR
> H.C. PHILLIPS
> THE HAMPSHIRE REGIMENT
> 8TH SEPTEMBER 1940 AGED 41

> 832719 PRIVATE
> A.J. SCOVELL
> THE HAMPSHIRE REGIMENT
> 8TH SEPTEMBER 1940

We cannot talk about either one of these soldiers here without the other, because as you can see, they were both from the same regiment and died on the same day. Unfortunately this was no coincidence. Both men were in the 2nd Battalion of the Hampshire Regiment and as the *Louth Standard* reports at the time, these soldiers were victims of an accidental explosion. This was the first military funeral that took place in Mablethorpe during the Second World War. The two soldiers were buried side by side.[16] Modern newspapers can also offer us information as to what happened too. *The Lincolnshire Echo* in 1994 ran a feature in their 'Gossiper' section regarding the soldiers and Mablethorpe; they spoke to a gentleman that was there on the day of the men's funeral, and the article states that the explosion was a blast at the recently laid minefield at Sandhills just up the coast from Mablethorpe.[17]

> 1624637 SERGEANT
> A.M. DOWESE
> NAVIGATOR/WIRELESS OPERATOR
> ROYAL AIR FORCE
> 1st NOVEMBER 1944 AGE 20

From the war records that are available, we know that Sergeant Arthur Michael Dowse was part of the 6th Operational Training Unit Coastal Command of the RAF Volunteer Reserve and was based at Silloth, Cumbria. Sergeant Dowse was killed when his plane crashed during a training flight at Silloth. He was flying in a Wellington MP680, a medium to long-distance bomber aircraft.[18] The funeral of Sergeant Dowse was reported in the *Louth Standard* on 11 November 1944.

The article gives us information about where he trained, went to school, and information about his family and their farm. From the probate records we know that Sergeant Dowse also left to his father £621 0s 2d.[19]

During this search a small piece of family history came to light. The *Louth Standard* of 1944 mentions that Arthur lost his brother following a lightning strike at the family farm. But this was not the only time that the family farm was struck by lightning. The *Louth Standard* of 7 September 1946 states that the family farm had been struck by lighting for a *third* time, and that the first time was thirty-five years earlier.[20]

It seems to be a magnet for lightning.

There are a few surprises to be found among the CWGC stones in St Mary the Virgin churchyard Heacham, Norfolk too.

There are two gravestones in Heacham churchyard that have both a personal stone and a Commonwealth War Grave. The CWGC stones are the same as the others with the details they provide, however, the personal graves have a greater amount of detail. This might be because of the way their deaths occurred.

## AIRMAN'S DEATH

### Mablethorpe Family Bereaved

IT IS WITH deepest regret we record the death on active service of Sgt.-Navigator A. Michael Dowse, R.A.F., the 20 year old only surviving son of Mr. and Mrs. Arthur Dowse, of Mile Lane, Mablethorpe.

The greatest sympathy will go out to the parents and his only sister in their tragic loss, the second they have sustained in a few years for, about four years ago, the elder son, Robert, whilst working on the farm, was struck dead by lightning.

Sgt. Dowse was born at Mablethorpe and after attending the Council School later went to Alford Grammar School, where he was a brilliant pupil, having a natural aptitude for drawing and draughtsmanship. When the Air Training Corps was formed, he joined the local Flight and later, although he could have remained on his father's farm, volunteered for the R.A.F. He completed his training in Canada, where he graduated as a Sergt.-Navigator in February of this year. He had almost completed his training and was due to join his squadron.

Unassuming to a degree, he was popular at School, in his A.T.C. Flight, and among his comrades of the R.A.F., and his tragic death will be heard of with regret by all who knew him.

*Newspaper article, A Dowse funeral* Louth Standard *11th November 1944, British Newspaper Archive.*

```
TR10/ 158270 PRIVATE
    F.W.A. GRAVER
     THE QUEENS
10TH AUGUST 1918 AGED 18
```

Private Gravers personal stone reads:

*'In loving memory of Pte Frederick William Arundel Graver 52nd Queens R.W.S. Rgt who was killed accidentally by an aeroplane while on leave Aug 10th, 1918, aged 18 years.'*

*Three Commonwealth War Graves from St Mary the Virgin churchyard, Heacham, Norfolk.*

This accident was reported in the newspapers at the time and an inquest was held. Private Graver was on leave and went on a family outing with his father on their pony-trap. When he returned, he offered to take the pony back to the pasture; he rode the pony and his sister followed behind on her bike. A little earlier a military plane had crashed in the field nearby and a second plane had come to check whether the pilot was alright. After this the pilot, Captain Morrice, took off but then experienced engine trouble and started his descent back to the field over the hedges, where visibility was poor. The underside of the plane hit Private Graver and the pony, who were both killed instantly; unfortunately this was witnessed by his sister. The coroner and jury, after hearing the statements of witnesses and Captain Morrice, returned a verdict of Accidental Death, which exonerated Captain Morrice of blame.[21]

> Lt ARTHUR BURELL THORNE
> ROYAL AIR FORCE
> 8th MAY 1918

Lt Arthur Burnell Thorne's personal stone reads:

> 'Sacred to the memory of Lt Arthur Burrell Thorne RFA Attd. RAF Killed in a collision in the air May 8th 1918 aged 23 years.'

The CWGC grave only details the information of his enlistment when he died. But his personal stone gives us a vast amount of information which allows us then to find him in the records. Arthur Thorne's RAF Officers' service record states that he joined the Royal Field Artillery in 1916. He was wounded by a gun shot in France on 25 June 1917. He was then unfit for service and was sent to Hillington Hall Military Hospital to continue his treatment. When fit, he then transferred to the RAF on 1 April 1918. This record also gives us the name of his next of kin and his permanent address which was The Willows, Heacham.[22] This tells us where he was living at the start of the war and the possibility of where his family lived between the 1911 and the 1921 census. Arthur died on 8 May 1918 along with two other comrades. He was a pilot flying with the 64th Training Squadron in a RE8 2-seater plane.[23]

The national and local newspapers of the time give details of the accident shortly after it happened. The *Pall Mall Gazette* (London), *Lancashire Evening Post*, *Hartlepool Northern Daily Mail*, *Birmingham Evening Dispatch* and the *Wester Times* (Exeter Devon) all ran the same article on 9 May 1918, just with a slight difference in the title. It read:

> An East Midland coroner was today notified of an aerial collision resulting in the deaths of Flight-Lieutenant Arthur Burell Thorne, twenty-three, Flight Second Lieutenant Mayer John Levine, nineteen, and Howard Watson, nineteen years of age. Flying at a great height from a Lincolnshire aerodrome, the two machines collided, became locked, and turned over crashing to the ground.

This was a tragic accident that occurred not on the battlefield but at home. From his military information I was able to find his probate record, in which he left his wife Katherine Gwenllian Thorne £551 3s 7d.[24]

Even though aeroplanes had only been around for about a decade before the start of the Great War both sides knew that they would need to control the skies during the war. But these two war stories show us how relatively new and unpredictable this invention still was.

---

PEYTON SHELDON HADLEY
NORTHAMPTONSHIRE REG
CAPTAIN M.C.
Born      Died
27 March 1895    25 Oct 1918

Captain Hadley is listed in the CWGC register and website, but his stone was erected by his family and has a more personal touch to it, stating when he was born as well as when he died. The information that we can get from the CWGC register and his gravestone paint a picture of the role that Captain Hadley had in the war. The CWGC register tells us that Captain Hadley was the son of W.S. Hadley, Master of Pembrook College Cambridge, and that he had a wife, Edith. It also states that he died of pneumonia following wounds he had received; he was 23 years old.[25] With the information from the register I was able to find out a great deal about Captain Hadley, who was an alumnus of Saint Ronan's School in Kent, which he joined in the scholarship class in 1906. He excelled in sports and kept in touch with his old school, writing to them in 1915. They have a large biography of his life at the school and beyond on their website.[26] His gravestone also tells us that he was a decorated soldier. He received the Military Cross for distinguished service in the field.[27] Through the 'Lives of the First World War' project at the Imperial War Museum, I was able to find out a little bit more about how Captain Hadley died. He was invalided home due to his injuries, but sadly died of influenza at the Central Military Hospital Eastbourne.[28]

> 69615 PRIVATE
> LEONARD JOHN DENNIS
> ROYAL DEFENCE CORPS
> 2nd FEBRUARY 1918 AGED 23

According to the 1911 census Leonard John Dennis was a farm labourer before the war.[29] Leonard was part of the 202 Protection company in the Royal Defence Corps, whose role it was to protect infrastructure such as ports, bridges and factories in Britain, and to guard military and prisoner of war camps. Leonard died at the 4th Scottish General Hospital in Glasgow from wounds he received in battle, and his effects were left to his father William Dennis in the sum of £10 1s 8d.[30]

> E G J FOWLE
> STOKER 1st CLASS R. N
> C/KX 122579
> H.M.L. C.P. (L) I
> 18th JULY 1943 AGE 25

Edmund George James Fowle was a Stoker 1st class in the Royal Navy. As a Stoker he worked and specialised in the engine rooms of the ships. The term Stoker derived from when the ships were coal fuelled and a Stoker shovelled coal into the boilers. During the Second World War many of the ships had been converted to oil fuel, but as this ran low some ships were converted back to coal. The Navy death records states that he died on active service at Stokes Bay Norfolk.[31] *The Lynn Advertiser* ran his obituary on 6 August 1943; it described how he was killed on a training exercise and that he had been a stoker in the Royal Navy for one and a half years. It gives details of a letter that the Rear Admiral sent to Edmund's parents which says that 'Stoker Fowle helped maintain the high traditions of the Royal Navy'. There is also a picture of Stoker Fowle,[32] turning a name on a gravestone into a real person, which in many cases we are unable to do. Before the war, according to the 1939 Register, Edmund worked as a dairy van driver,[33] a fact further confirmed in his obituary in *The Lynn Advertiser*.

> 655230 SERGEANT
> R.T. FRARY
> ROYAL AIR FORCE
> 14th AUGUST 1943 AGED 24

I have been able to find Sergeant Reginald Thomas Frary in some military records because of his service number and in the local newspapers.

*Obituary for E Fowle,* Lynn Advertiser *6th August 1943, British Newspaper Archive.*

Sergeant Frary was part of the 7th Operational Training Unit coastal command at the military base Limavady County, Londonderry, Northern Ireland.[34] *The Yorkshire Post and Leeds Intelligencer* ran a very tiny piece on the death of Sergeant Frary on 17 August 1943, stating that he had died and that he was a wireless operator–air gunner, and that he was from Southend House, Bramley, Leeds.[35] This little bit of information as to where he lived allowed me to find his marriage in the local papers. The *Lynn Advertiser* of 4 June 1943 gives us a glimpse into their special day. Sergeant Frary married Betty Lambert in St Peters Church, Leeds, in June 1943. The newspaper describes the dresses that the bride and bridesmaids wore, and lists relations of the couple including Sergeant Frary's sister Doris.[36] This is good to know, because on 1921 census Reginald Frary (who was only 2 years old at the time) was not living with his direct family but was instead listed as a 'lodger'.[37] From the probate records we can see that Sergeant Frary left £183 15s to his widow Betty.[38] He had been married for only three months before he died. His grave is in St Mary's churchyard Heacham, Norfolk, because that is where he and his parents are from.

> 2ND LIEUTENANT
> EUSTACE ROLFE
> GUNTHER M.A.
> ROYAL ARTILLERY
> 31ST MAY 1940 AGED 37

Eustace Rolfe Gunther started as a Sapper and was with the 72nd Searchlight Regiment Royal Artillery. He was made a 2nd Lieutenant in March 1939 as reported in *The London Gazette*.[39] He was not killed overseas nor by the enemy, he was accidentally shot in Norfolk and died from his wounds. The coroner records the death as 'died from a gunshot wound caused by a rifle inadvertently discharged'.[40]

> 13002874 PRIVATE
> W.A. SKEET
> PIONEER CORPS
> 26th MAY 1941 AGED 43

What caught my attention about the gravestone of William Albert Skeet was his age. A quick calculation tells me that William was born 1897/8 which means that he was old enough to have also taken part in the First World War and survived. William was part of the 1/5 Norfolk Regiment, and his service numbers were 4332 and 240931. He received the Victory and the British Medal at the end of the First World War. Between the wars William married Matilda Rowe in 4th Quarter of 1920.[41] The *Lynn Advertiser* on 6 June 1941 reported on Private Skeet's funeral and gives us more of an insight into the man and his involvement in the wars and, tragically, also his death:

> Mr Skeet was unscathed through the 1914–18 war. On the outbreak of the present war he was the first man in Heacham to Volunteer, joined the Pioneer Corps, and within a few weeks was again in France. He was safely evacuated from Dunkirk, and later served in several parts of England. In a German raid on the south-west town he was injured by a blast of a bomb, and on May 26th died in a Cornish Sanatorium.[42]

William Skeet had two children and on 26 May 1944 they, along with their mother, remembered their father again in the *Lynn Advertiser*:

> SKEET– In ever-loving memory of a dear husband and dad. Private William Albert Skeet died through enemy action in Cornwall, May 26th 1941. With only memories left to keep, without farewell he sleep: sleep on, dear-one. God knows best, on earth there's strife in Heaven rest.
> –From a loving wife and daughter Daphne, Heacham.

> SKEET – In ever loving memory of my dear Dad. Private William Skeet, died through enemy action in Cornwall, May 26th 1941. Sweet be your rest dear dad. Tis sweet to breathe your name. In life I loved you dearly. In death I do the same.
> From his loving son George Merchant Navy, somewhere at sea.[43]

Private William Skeet survived so much through both wars and was lovingly remembered by his family.

## Personal Military Gravestones

Personal graves are erected by the families that are left behind, and as you will see they can leave us a vast amount of information – sometimes even more than the records.

In St Mary's churchyard Appledore, Devon, is the gravestone of Thomas Harris and his two sons. All three were lost in the First World War:

'...who were lost at sea on the Schooner P.T Harris during the Great War June 1916 'Thomas Harris Master Mariner aged 41 years Thomas Leonard aged 16 William aged 14.'

The stone was erected by his wife. From the details on the stone, I was able to find them in the Death at Sea 1891–1972 records which state that all three 'men' (even though William was 14 and Thomas 16) were 'supposedly' drowned off the Irish coast 4 July 1916. It also states that the ship 'supposedly' sank.[44] This means they have never recovered the vessel nor, unfortunately, the bodies. In the *Huddersfield Daily Examiner* of 30 August 1916, the vessel was logged as overdue and that it had sailed from Glasgow for St Brieuc on 29 June.[45] This must have been an agonising time for the families back home.

Also in St Mary's Appledore is the commemoration to William Alexander who *'died in Mesopotamia whilst serving king and country June 20th 1917 aged 19'*.

*Gravestone of Wesley and Henry Tuck St Nicholas churchyard, Dersingham, Norfolk.*

This is written at the bottom of his parents grave. Even with just these few details I was able to find that he also has a Commonwealth War grave in Basra War Cemetery in Iraq. His name and details are listed on panel number 15 along with other fallen soldiers from the Devonshire Regiment. He was part of the 1st/6th Battalion.[46]

In St Nicholas churchyard Dersingham, Norfolk, is the gravestone of two brothers: Wesley Edgar Ruben Tuck and Hubert Henry Tuck.

*'In Loving memory of Wesley Edgar Ruben Tuck 15671 9th Norfolk died Oct 24th aged 25 years. Also Hubert Henry 60002 21st Canadians died Sept 16th aged 27 years Interred at British Cemetery Puchevillers (France) both fell at capture of (Courcelette) Sept 15th 1916 3rd and 4th sons of Frederick James and Julia Tuck of Dersingham.'*

This personal gravestone gives us a vast amount of information. It tells us that Wesley was part of the 9th Norfolk Regiment 15671 and Hubert the 21st Canadians 60002. This information has allowed for a deeper look into the personal and military lives of these two brothers. Wesley's war service record has survived, if hard to read in parts, and tells us that before the war he was a shop assistant and that he served at home from 18 September 1914 to 29 August 1915, after that he was transferred to France where he served from 30 August 1915 to 24 August 1016, the time of his death. During that time, he was wounded on three separate occasions. On the third he was transferred to hospital in Oxford, where he died of his wounds. From the records we know that he was awarded the 1914–15 Star, the British War Medal and the Victory Medal, because his record holds the receipts. The amazing thing about service records is that they also give a description of the man at the time of joining. From this we know that Wesley was 5ft 10inches and had dark brown hair and brown eyes with a fresh complexion.[47]

Hubert Henry Tuck was in Canada at the outbreak of war, because he travelled to Montreal, Canada, from Liverpool in 1909 on the ship *Corsian* of the Allan Line Steamship Co.[48] From his gravestone we know that he was part of the Canadian Army. The First World War Canadian service records for Hubert Henry Tuck survive in remarkable condition with twenty-eight pages for Hubert alone. It tells us that when he joined on 22 March 1915, he was 5ft 8 inches tall with blue eyes and brown hair, and he had two teeth missing with two 'defective', but that these were classed as 'slight' defects and not a cause for rejection. We also know that he had been a salesman prior to joining up. During his time in France, it was recorded that he was treated for a bout of influenza between 17 and 23 October 2015, after which he rejoined his regiment. He was then treated at the Canadian Field Ambulance for cuts to his thumb on 5 February 2016, and for defective vision again at the Canadian Field Ambulance from 1 to 4 May 2016 where once again he rejoined his regiment. Hubert Henry Tuck died on 16 September 1916 at the Forty-Four Casualty Clearing Station and his records state only that he died of his wounds.[49] The gravestone tells us that he is buried in Puchevillers British Cemetery. This is also confirmed on the CWGC register; his grave is in Plot 3 Row D Grave 4.[50]

In St Mary's churchyard Heacham, Norfolk, is the grave of Alfred Bird.

> '*In loving memory of Charles Bird son of John and Mary Ann Bird died May 20th 1896 aged 4 year. Also Alfred Bird 3rd Dragoon Guards Killed in Action Arras April 11th 1917 aged 20 years.*'

The stone was initially place for his brother Charles, who died at the age of 4; Alfred's details were added to the bottom of the stone. As the grave also has the names of his parents and brother, I was able to find him on the 1911 census where Alfred was 14 and a 'paperboy'.[51] Alfred was a Private in Household Cavalry Regiment of the 3rd Dragoon Guards. His regiment number was 8067. He was Killed in Action in France and Flanders.[52] His name is also listed on the Commonwealth Arras War Memorial Bay 1 in France.

What links these graves is the involvement of the deceased in war. The personal stones represent the desire for living relatives to leave lasting evidence of how their family members died and to ensure they would not be forgotten. The CWGC graves were, and still are, an act of national remembrance so that no man or woman should be forgotten.

*Chapter 5*

# HOW PEOPLE DIED

Human beings are curious and like to know the answers of how and why, it's in our nature. We love a good mystery. You can see that in the popularity of crime novels and dramas. Knowing how a person died gives the living closure and peace. The gravestones of our ancestors can give us clues into the mystery of how they died because they have it written on their monument. This, however, is not something that is seen on gravestones today. From my personal experience, people today would rather be remembered as they were when they were young and healthy, rather than by the suffering they endured and their eventual end. So, why did our ancestors want to leave these details after they were gone?

I have come across many different types of death details, some I expected, others I did not.

**Illness**

As you might expect, illness is the most common form of death present on gravestones. What is interesting, however, is the way it is expressed. There seems to be a great deal of difference between the portrayals of men and women who died from illness.

The table below shows the types of language used and to which gender.

| Male | Female |
|---|---|
| After a short but distressing affliction | After a long and painful affliction which was borne with patience and fortitude |
| After a long and severe affliction | After suffering a long and painful decline with patience and fortitude |

| Male | Female |
|---|---|
| After years of patient suffering | Who after bearing a long and trying illness with exemplary patience |
| After a lingering illness | A long and severe affliction borne with Christian fortitude |
| Who after a long and painful illness which he bore with Christian fortitude | Who after being long but happily trained in the school of affliction finished well |
| Died after a few hours illness | |
| Who after many months of protracted illness expired | |

The female dedications have a large emphasis on the suffering of the deceased and how they endured it. The male dedications on the other hand are rather more blunt in expression. Why is this? What can the difference in these dedications tell us about our ancestors?

The Victorians followed the evangelical ideas of a 'good death', where the family were able to gather around to hear a person's last words and tie up all loose ends, and the dying be able to make peace with God. Therefore, a long, slow drawn-out death, such as tuberculosis, was seen as 'ideal'. This type of death was also romanticised in novels of the period, such Helen Burns in Charlotte Bronte's *Jane Eyre* (1847), and Bessy Higgins in Elizabeth Gaskell's *North and South* (1854–55); the paleness and thin figure caused by tuberculosis was perceived by the upper classes as 'beautiful'. Illness, especially for women, was seen as inevitable; they were the ones who nursed the sick and were responsible for them. For upper- and middle-class women the subject of their own health was a constant discussion. In her book *The Victorian House*, Judith Flanders discusses this, and the fact that many women made the illnesses their own, calling them 'my' headaches for example. The illnesses and afflictions became part of their identity. However, the romanticised view and what was portrayed on the stones compared to the reality was rather different. Death was everywhere and tuberculosis is a nasty disease – there is nothing romantic about it. The wording used in these dedications indicated the Christian piety of the women, and this was certainly expected of them in life and was a treat that they wanted to carry with them into death. Christian piety is no different for the male dedications, but the males were the head of the household, strong, the breadwinners for their family. The dedications are short and concise with no frills. Many of the male dedications were also followed by details about their life and achievements. These were just as important, it seems, to their identity as was their piety.

There have been a few stones that state a specific illness. The first of these was in All Saints' churchyard Leicester.

> 'To the Memory of George Green late of this parish who fell victim to a rapid and incurable consumption on 29th day of April 1815 aged 37 years. Leaving a wife and four children to lament the loss of a tender husband and indulgent parent.'

Consumption, or tuberculosis as we know it, in the Georgian period killed more people than any other disease. In 1815 when George died, one in four recorded deaths were from tuberculosis. It was highly infectious as it was passed through the air by coughing, and the statement that George Green made was rather accurate – it was rapid and incurable.

A stone in the churchyard of St Margaret's Church Leicester states a family dying from smallpox. The stone is dedicated to William Curtis and his wife Sarah and it says:

> 'To the memory of William Curtis and Sarah his wife, both from Tugby in this county, and while discharging offices of parental affection dealing with the afflictions of a daughter fell of smallpox of which they died he the 20th Oct 1798 aged 66 she the 21st Oct 1798 aged 63 years.'

They both died within a day of each other. This stone clearly shows how quickly that disease can sweep through a family. I have a more in-depth look at the subject of smallpox and this gravestone in Chapter 2.

The stone of Joshua Bignell, which originally stood in the churchyard of St Martin's Leicester, is now located in Saffron Hill Cemetery on the outskirts of Leicester due to the remodelling of St Martins Churchyard and reads:

> 'To the memory of Joshua Bignell Jnr of Croydon Surrey Head Groom to T. Bainbridge, Esqre who after a few days affliction of Erysipelas departed this life 28th November 1839 27th year of his age.'

Erysipelas, also known as St Anthony's Fire, was a bacterial infection that affected the skin causing hot red rashes, usually from a mild wound, stings or scratches. Today we know this to be a streptococcal infection. In the 1830s, however, without the aid of antibiotics the only way they

*Gravestone of George Green All Saints' churchyard Leicester.*

could treat this was by cleaning the skin and cold compresses, which as you can imagine was largely unsuccessful.[1]

With medical advances we know that there are many more illnesses that would have been present, but these are the ones that have specifically been mentioned.

## Accidents

Accidents happen, it's a fact of life. Today, however, we are governed by health and safety legislation, protective equipment and common sense gained from better knowledge across all areas of work and leisure. However, even with all our safety precautions, accidents still occur. The Georgian and Victorian periods were the ages of innovation and industrial revolution, with the birth and expansion of mechanised machines for mass production, factories, steam railways and boats, cars, household time-saving devices, medical advances, telecommunications, and infrastructures with new materials. But, as with all new advances, with them comes risk, so it is not surprising that one of the highest causes of death after infection in previous eras was accidents.

Any sudden, unnatural, or unexplained deaths were supposed to be reported, investigated, and an inquest held by the coroner and a jury, to determine if any criminal act occurred and the cause of death. This produced a coroner's report, and the inquest was also very often written about in the local papers. However, in the nineteenth century coroners' procedures struggled to keep pace with the increase in unexplained deaths due to urbanisation, industrialisation, and a growing population. By 1850 local magistrates were forced to restrict the number of inquests held in some urban areas. Therefore, it may be that the gravestone is the only indication of what happened.

Again, as we did with women and childbirth in Chapter 2, we have statistical evidence from Guys Hospital in London, which kept a record of the types and number of accidental deaths by J.C. Steele *Numerical Analysis of Patients treated at Guys Hospital for the last seven years, from 1854 to 1861*. This recorded the number of people treated in Guys Hospital for accidents. However, for incidents to be recorded people need to be physically present at the hospital, or someone needed to notify the right departments. In the table of accidental deaths, it lists: burns, clothes catching fire; heated fluids; explosion of gas; fall from height; fall of heavy weight; accidental poisoning; gunshot wounds; machinery accidents; railway accidents; accidents on the river, in large barges or shipboard. All of these are associated with the rapid pace of the changes that were happening within industries and societies.[2]

*Three graves of drowning burials St Mary's churchyard Appledore, Devon.*

The last one listed – 'accidents on the river, in barges or shipboard' – is a hard one to record as many of the people lost in this way may never be found nor go to hospital. This is where what is written on the gravestones can help.

In the churchyard of St Mary's Appledore, on the north Devon coast, this type of death is very prominent on the graves. Appledore is a seafaring and shipbuilding community, and it is still home to these skills today. Many of the men who are buried in the churchyard drowned or were lost at sea.

We know this because they tell us:

> 'In memory of John George beloved son of Albert and Janie Vaggers who accidentally drowned June 17th, 1928 aged 23 years'.

John George came from a family of boatmen and was unfortunately lost when he was taking a visitor, Henry Gordon Gilbert, for a sail from Appledore. An inquest was held into the death and the coroner ruled that he accidentally drowned.[3]

> 'Sacred to the memory of William Guard Master Mariner who was drowned off Bude on the 7th March 1877 age 57 years. Also in memory of his three brothers who were lost at sea John Guard Stephenson Guard Thomas Guard.'

William Guard went to sea as boy in April 1840 he was 5ft 4inches and could neither read nor write.[4] He then progressed through until he was a Master Mariner. The *Echo London* of 7 March 1877 reported the loss of the ship *Maria*, of which William Guard was master, and told us that the *Maria* was bound for Boscastle with coals and ran in the back of the breakwater at Bude and immediately began to break up. The mate of the ship was saved but not unfortunately William Guard.[5] Without any dates or other information regarding William's brothers I believe it is safe to assume that their bodies were never recovered and therefore exact dates may not be known.

> 'John Burgess was drowned at sea May 22nd 1862 aged 52 years.'

Unfortunately, there is little evidence for this accident in the historical documents and possibly he was never found. So without the gravestones this information may never have been known in the future.

> 'In loving memory of Thomas E Fishwick who was drowned in the River Torridge February 19th 1910 aged 41 years.'

Thomas Fishwick and two other men died when the boat they were sailing in capsized. The newspapers also report on the accident and give us a glimpse into the lives they left behind. Thomas was sailing in the estuary of the rivers Taw and Torridge, where ferries ran between Appledore and Instow. On the day in question Thomas Fishwick was travelling across the estuary with two other experienced boatmen, William Bailey and Albert Vaggers, and two passengers. The weather had been 'boisterous' and shortly after the boat set sail onlookers stated that it was caught in a sudden squall and the boat had capsized. The two passengers were lost before help could arrive, but Albert Vaggers, William Bailey and Thomas Fishwick were able to hang on. Albert and William were recovered, but unfortunately Thomas was not. The report also tells us that Thomas Fishwick was survived by his wife and nine children (although they had had fourteen children born to them in total).[6] Albert Vaggers was the father of the above mentioned John Vaggers, who also tragically drowned some years later in 1928.

> 'In loving memory of John Cann the beloved husband of Arabella Cann who drowned in the River Taw March 3rd 1890.'

John Cann and his sons were fishermen, and he was drowned while out dragging seaweed from Western Beach, which they would then sell to farmers for manure. John Cann was in the boat with his son-in-law Richard Taylor, who also drowned in the accident. They had loaded their boat 'Betsy' too high with seaweed and the sea was choppy due to the

> Strangely enough, John Cann narrowly escaped drowning during the late salmon season. His party were shooting a net at Greysand, and while the net was being taken out he stood on shore holding the rope. The river current caught the net, and as by some mischance Cann had got the rope twisted round him, he was thrown off his feet and dragged into the water. Mr. T. Fishwick happened to be near, and, coming to the rescue, saved the man. This tragedy ought to be a warning to the men of Appledore not to be so rash as to load their boats to sinking point in future.

*Newspaper article of John Cann's first escape in the* Western Times *5th March 1890, British Newspaper Archive.*

meeting of the tides; the waves broke over the boat and sank it. John Cann left a widow and seven children, although mostly grown up, and also three orphans – children of his brother whom he had adopted. The accident was reported in great detail in the *Western Times* 5 March 1890, it also gives information on another accident involving John Cann.

In this instance John Cann was rescued from drowning by Thomas Fishwick, who we have already met via the gravestones. The article ends with a warning to other fisherman of Appledore not to load their boats to sinking point in the future.[7]

These are just a fraction of the stones that are dedicated in the churchyard to men who have drowned or been lost at sea. These stones give us a snapshot of the devastating effect this can have on a family and a community; we know that some of these men, and their families, knew each other. This way of life was fundamental to the men in this community, and generation after generation they returned to the sea to earn a living, leaving the women behind to wait, to worry and sadly, to mourn.

Accidents also occurred on and around the ships too. St Mary's Appledore also has the stones of John Bale Evely and Pearson C. Adams.

> 'In loving memory of John Bale Evely who was killed Dec 11th 1906 interred in Gloucester cemetery until day break.'

On the face of it the stone of John Evely doesn't give us that much information; however, by knowing that he was killed and interred in Gloucester I was able to find out that John died because of an accident on board the *Mary Fanny*, where he sustained a fractured skull as detailed in the Deaths at Sea Records.[8] The newspapers of the day give us a few more details about how this happened. The *Gloucester Citizen* on the 17 December 1906 states that John fell in the hold of the ship and was subsequently taken to Gloucester Infirmary.[9] This was where he died of to his injuries and was then buried.

> 'Erected by the crews of the Diving Cutters 'Ann Eltbeth' and 'Pomp' [of Whitstable] in memory of Pearson C Adams [one of their crew] who died July 4th 1871 from injuries received on board the wreck 'Brenda' from Lundy Island to Appledore aged 19 years.'

The stone of Pearson Adams gives us a vast amount of information to delve into. From the 1871 census record we know that Pearson was aboard the ship *Ann Elizabeth* along with the crew, who erected the monument on the night of Sunday 2 April.[10] Pearson Adams and the crew were part of the team that were lifting the wreck of the *Brenda* which had sunk off Lundy Island. *The Western Daily Press* gives the details of the wreck and the lifting of the vessel which was the first wreck ever to be raised from Lundy Island.[11] The *North Devon Journal* gives details of Pearson Adams' accident. Pearson was one of the divers raising the wreck and 'whilst assisting had his leg broken and other injuries by the bit of the windlass being broken by the tow rope'. Pearson was taken to the Royal George Inn in Appledore where he received surgical assistance, and it was found that he had also received internal injuries which then led to his death.[12]

It was not just people working on the boats who suffered, accidents happened even to those who used boats for pleasure, as can be seen in the churchyard of All Saints' churchyard Rampton Nottinghamshire.

> *'In loving memory of Henry Hurst who was drowned at Yarmouth July 28th 1887 aged 35 years Also of Selena Hurst his wife who was drowned at the same time aged 27 years.'*

This husband and wife, who were from London but staying in Yarmouth, were travelling on a boat called the *Dawn of Day* when it was involved in an accident with another boat; ten people drowned between the two boats. At the inquest of these ten people the jury reached the verdict regarding the *Dawn of Day*, stating that the accident was 'unavoidable'.[13] All of this was reported in the local papers and in London.

It is not surprising that these types of deaths are listed as these are coastal towns. But this type of death is not just found on the coast.

In All Saints' churchyard Leicester, I came across a gravestone of two brothers: William Wilkinson, 19 years old, and Richard Wilkinson, 13 years old. These two brothers had gone swimming in the canal. The stone reads:

> *'This monitor of human instability is erected by their companions and friends to record the untimely end of two affectionate brothers William Charles Wilkinson aged 19 years and Richard aged 13, (sons of William Charles Wilkinson and Jane his wife) who on the fifth of August 1850 while bathing near St Mary's Mill sunk together to rise no more. Lovely and pleasant in their lives and in their death too were not divided.'*

This gives us far more information than just burial details. This is very much a case of the living remembering the dead as it was their friends and not their family who erected the monument, and they wanted future generations to know this. The extent of the details on the stone also can serve as a warning to others of the dangers of swimming near St Mary's Mill. From the burial record we can see that both boys were living at Duke Street, Leicester.[14]

It is not just children that can fall foul of this. In St George's churchyard Leicester is the gravestone of Elizabeth Knight Brown who was 'accidentally drowned Feb 18th 1891 interred March 26th 1891 in the 59th year of her age.' The *Leicester Chronicle* on 26 and 28 March 1891 report the coroner's findings with the titles: 'Drowned in Fog' and 'River Bank Unprotected'. The coroner ruled it as an accidental death, that the river had no barrier and Elizabeth fell to her death. He also made recommendations for improvements to the area.[15]

In All Saints' churchyard Loughborough, Leicestershire, there is a gravestone to three men. The stone is rather damaged and lying on its back, but it has left us with a powerful message regarding the dangers and specifically uses the word 'warning', for the dangers of swimming in rivers and what can happen when you try to rescue people too. The stone for these three men was erected by voluntary subscription, which means that the people of their community gave what they could to erect the monument.

> *'Here in the same grave the bodies of Thomas BOMBROFFE aged 46 William PECK aged 23 William SMITH aged 18 all of this parish who were unfortunately drowned together in the River Soar on the ninth day of July 1767.'It is prsumed* [sic] *that Bombroffe lost his life by endeavouring to save his two companions for he only was found in his cloths* [sic]. *Some principal inhabitants of this parish tenderly concerned for the sudden fate of those their fellow Christians and for perpetual warning a* [as inscribed] *Hothers caused this stone to be erected by voluntary subscription.'*

Another element of Dr Steele's statistics for which I have found evidence is collisions with street vehicles. In the churchyard of St Margaret's Leicester is the stone of William Pringle.

> *'Sacred to the memory of William Henry Pringle who whilst on his journey for the house of Messers Holme, Wilson and Co of London was thrown from his gig in the Belgrave Gate in this town and killed on the spot the 26th of March 1834 35 years leaving a wife and seven children to deplore his loss.'*

For the family historian this stone is the diamond in the rough. It has details of his death, the how the when and where, who he worked for, and about the people he left behind. If there are no historical documents about this accident, then the stone gives us the story. As it happens, we are lucky that the *Leicester Journal* on 28 March 1834 reported the coroner's inquest into the death. The article states that William Pringle was a wine and sprit merchant from Thames Street London and gives the statements of what happened from two 'Gentlemen witnesses'. It says that while travelling down Belgrave Gate at some speed, William's gig collided with a hand truck that was partly in the causeway and partly in the road; William was then flung from his gig and died on impact to the ground. The coroner concluded an accidental death. However, he did fine the owner of the hand cart and recommended that these not be left on a great thoroughfare such as Belgrave Gate.[16]

## Death by Burning

In the churchyard of St Mary's Snettisham, Norfolk, is the grave of Mary Ann Harrod:

> 'This stone was erected by the teachers and children of Penrose Street School London In loving memory of Mary Ann the beloved wife of Henry Harrod she was accidentally burnt to death November 27th 1884 aged 32 years.'

Mary's husband Henry was the caretaker at the Penrose Board school and they both lived in a cottage near the school in Penrose Street. *The London Standard* reported the accident on 28 November 1884, and it transpired that Mary Ann fell asleep in front of the fire and a red-hot ember ignited her dress. Witnesses heard her scream and ran out into the street where they put the fire out, but she was burnt all over. The jury at the inquest returned a verdict of accidental death.[17] From the 1881 census we can see that Mary Ann and Henry were living at the board school with their three small children and that Mary Ann was born in Snettisham, which would explain why she is buried in Snettisham churchyard.[18]

> 'Here lies interred the body of Benjamin Hart who were unfortunately deprived of life by accident of fire after much pain and suffering he departed this life sept 1838 aged 55 years.'

This grave is in the churchyard of Breedon Priory Leicestershire. The cause of his death is backed up by his death certificate which states that he died from the 'effects of a burn'.[19] Unfortunately, at present there are no other accounts of the accident and what happened to Benjamin, so without the stone we may never have known this. We are lucky also that his death certificate has survived because at this point in time the recording of deaths and issuing of death certificates was only just beginning.

Death by fire was something I wasn't expecting but probably should have been. Open fires were still the norm in homes and it is probable that more people were hurt or died from this than we can imagine.

## Falls or fallen objects

The stone of Charles Robins in the churchyard of Breedon Priory is one of the stones that without the information on it, we would know very little about how he died:

> 'This stone is to the memory of Charles Robins late of Thringstone who was unfortunately kill'd by a fall from his horse August 11th 1781 aged 46 years.'

Charles's death occurred before death registration and certificates so without the stone we would not know what happened. However, what I have been able to find is the probate of his estate. Charles was a 'Victualler', which is a person who is licensed to sell alcohol. His probate gives us the breakdown of his possessions room by room, including a brewery and the sum once expenses are paid was then left to his widow. What this gives us though is a glimpse into how much a gravestone and a funeral would cost in 1781, as these were just some of the expenses listed. The gravestone was £3 4s 11d and the funeral was £17 4s.[20]

We can see from this that Charles Robins was not a poor man; not everyone would have been able to have – or to pay for – the kind of gravestone and funeral that he received. However, his relatives clearly wanted future generations to know that Charles fell from his horse over the fact that he was a victualler, an indication perhaps of the effect this accident had on them.

> 'In loving and affectionate remembrance of William Corah of Shepshed who died Jan 4th 1888 from injuries received by a fall of a stone at Hathern Parish Quarry Shepshed aged 51 years.'

This gravestone in St James the Greater Oaks in Charnwood, Leicestershire, gives us details of an accident at work which

*Probate record extract for C Robins of funeral and gravestone costs, www.findmypast.co.uk.*

unfortunately were all too common. The newspapers give us an insight into what happened. The inquest into William Corah's death was held at the Jolly Farmer's Inn in Shepshed and was reported by the *Nottingham Evening Post* on Friday 6 January 1888. It reports that on 23 December 1887, William was working with his son at the quarry loosening stone when a large block of about two tons fell on his back, and the loose stones that came with it fell on his leg and left foot crushing his foot. The surgeon removed the crushed part of his foot, but a week later William died from internal injuries received during the accident; this was also the result reached by the jury at the inquest.[21] From the newspaper report we can see that William was working with his son Samuel. Therefore, I was able to find his family on the 1881 census, when they were living at 11 Cabbage Row Sheepshed (Shepshed). Samuel was one of seven children born to William and his wife Hannah. According to the census, Arthur and Samuel were the elder two of William's three sons and followed their father as quarrymen.[22]

However, there are those stones that leave us with more questions than they answer. In the churchyard of St John the Baptist in the village of Grimston, Leicestershire, is the stone of William Lowe Sleath.

*'Sacred to the memory of William Lowe the dearly beloved son of Andrew and Anne Maria Sleath who was accidentally killed at Frickley Yorkshire November 13th 1890 aged 17 years and 8 months.'*

The family who erected this stone clearly wanted the reason for his death – 'accidentally killed in Frickley Yorkshire' – to be remembered. However, unlike the other graves we have seen the specific details are missing:

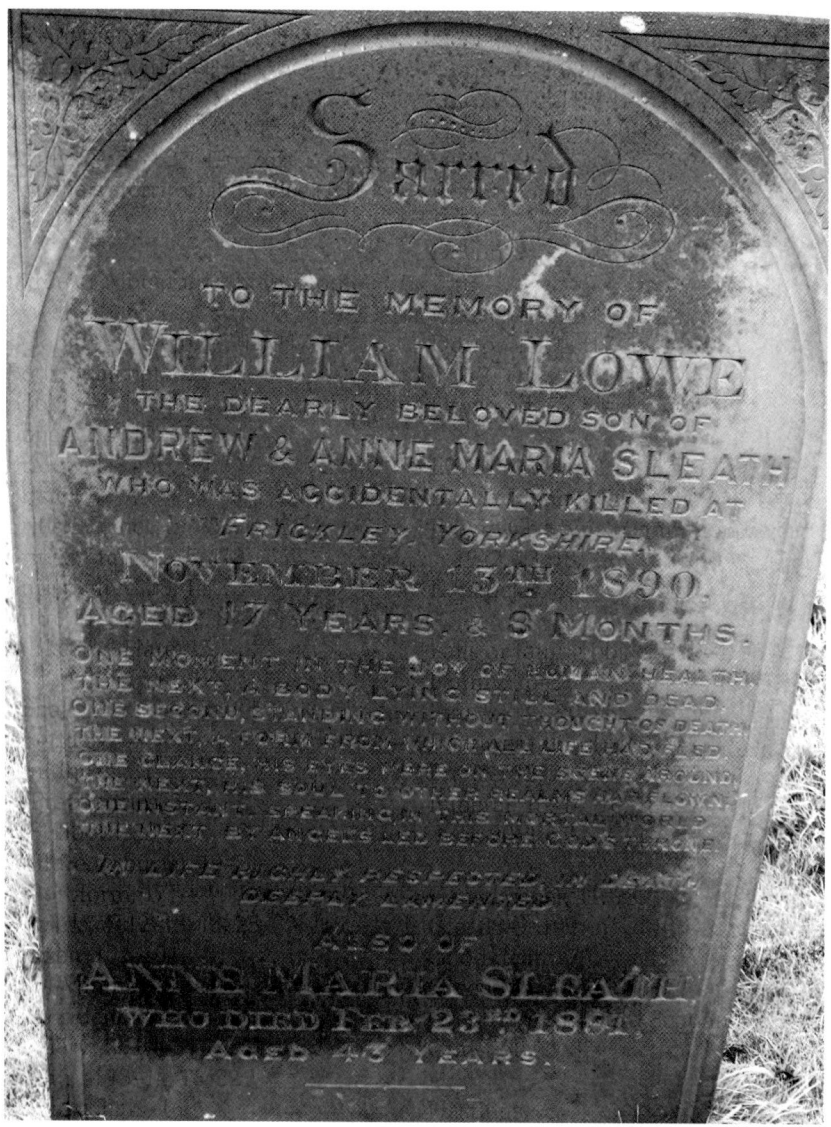

*Gravestone of William Lowe Sleath St John the Baptist churchyard Grimston Leicestershire.*

> **GRIMSTONE.**
>
> SHOCKING DEATH OF A NATIVE OF GRIMSTONE. —On Thursday last, a native of this village, named William Lowe Sleath, met with his death in a very terrible manner. It appears that he was employed as a porter at the Railway Station, Frickley, Yorkshire, and was knocked down by the Leeds express and cut to pieces, death being instantaneous. Deceased was a son of Mr. Andrew Sleath, and the body was removed to Grimstone for burial, the interment taking place on Sunday last in the presence of a large number of sympathising friends. The officiating clergyman was the Rev. Lefroy Baker, who read the beautiful burial service in a most impressive manner. The utmost sympathy is felt for the sorrowing parents and friends in their sad bereavement.

*Newspaper article for William Sleath* Melton Mowbray Times *21st November 1890, British Newspaper Archive.*

how did he die? The blanks would need to be filled by the historical documents, at least the details the stone has given us give a place to start. From this I was able to find a newspaper article in the *Sheffield Evening Telegraph* of 17 November 1890 about the inquest into his death. He was a porter at Frickley Railway Station and was run over by the Sheffield to Leeds express and killed instantly. The verdict was ruled as 'Accidentally Killed'. The *Melton Mowbray Times* also ran a small article about the accident as he was a native of Grimston, and gives details of his funeral and family ties.

A gravestone in St Mary in Arden churchyard Market Harborough, Leicestershire, has a stone that also follows a similar line:

> 'Sacred to the memory of William Eaglefield Hull who was killed by accident at Derby Station May 3rd 1861 in the 23rd year of his age.'

Again, William Hull was a porter at Derby train station and the accident had occurred when he tried to save a member of the public. *The Staffordshire Advertiser* on 8 May 1861 and the *Morning Post* (London) 11 May 1861 both report 'Shocking Accident'. William Hull was killed as he attempted to save a passenger who tried to board the train while it was moving, and the doors had been locked. In saving the man William Hull slipped and fell under the train; it was reported that all six carriages ran over him, and he was killed instantly.[23] William Hull's gravestone recognises that he was killed by accident, however it doesn't mention that he had saved another man, without the newspapers we may not have known.

## Coal Mining Accidents

Quarries and railways were not the only places where accidents happened. Coal mines were notoriously dangerous places for adults and children to work. While researching my own ancestors who were coal miners in Northumberland in the Seaton Delaval, Blyth and Morpeth areas, I came across the gravestones of quite a few people who all lost their lives due to accidents at the coal pits. The Durham mining museum website (www.dmm.org.uk) lists all the coal pits in the area. They also list the accidents and deaths that they know of that happened, along with grave details and inspection reports. This is a valuable resource and is where a lot of the information for the gravestones below has come from, but in some cases I was able to delve a little deeper with the help of local newspapers.

In the churchyard of St Mary's Horton, Northumberland, I came across a great number of graves where the cause of death was listed on the stones as accidents at various collieries. Below is a selection of these as there are far more than I can discuss here.

This is the grave of two brothers:

*'In memory of John the beloved son of John and Margaret Rhodes of Cowpen Square who was killed while driving from the shaft at the Isabella Pit May 8th, 1866 Aged 13 years'.*

*'In memory of Richard Davison Rhodes who was killed at the Isabella Pit Cowpen, by the Tyne, set No. 15 Decr. 4th 1872 Aged 12½ years.'*

Both brothers worked at the Isabella Pit at Cowpen Colliery near Blyth. This pit was sunk in 1848 and was closed in February 1966. The two brothers were some of the youngest workers to be allowed to work at the coal mines. In 1860 an Act for the Regulation and Inspection of Mines was passed. This stated that no boy under the age of 12 could be employed in mines and collieries.[24] Both boys would have fallen under this Act so would have only worked for a year and six months respectively. John was a 'Driver' and drove the horses pulling tubs on the main road underground. He was killed when a set of tubs he was driving up an incline jerked off the track; he was crushed against the wall and died of his injuries.[25] Richard was a screener, his job was to pass the coals over the screens into the waggons, and clean them from stones, slates, brasses. However, according to the *Newcastle Chronicle*, he was killed by a train of empty waggons passing over him on the waggon way at the Isabella Pit.[26] It is hard to imagine how the family would have felt at losing their child to a mining accident, and the situation they must have been in to allow a second son to work in the mine and losing him too.

> 'In affectionate remembrance of Humphrey Armstrong Burt beloved son of Anthony and Jane Burt who was killed at Bebside Colliery Nov 21st 1882 aged 17 years.'

Humphrey was a 'Putter' who fills the tubs with coal from the hewers and then pushes the tub from behind to the crane or shaft. He was killed by being crushed by a tub.

> 'In loving memory of ... Thomas Robson (Newton) their son died Dec 7th 1896 from burns accidentally received in New Delaval pit aged 14 years.'

Thomas was the son of Lancelot and Kate Newton. He is commemorated on the family stone underneath his sister Dora who died aged 8, with his parents inscribed beneath him. Thomas was a stone putter and his accident was reported in the *Morpeth Herald* on 12 December 1896 along with the inquest and its verdict. Thomas died of burns received from a gas explosion due to him carrying a naked flame just along the tunnel from where he was working. The coroner during the inquest questioned the witnesses quite harshly regarding the safety of the tunnel and whether the accident could have been prevented. The jury returned a verdict of death by fire-damp explosion and they recommended that in future more precautions should be made to prevent this happening again.[27]

> 'In affectionate remembrance of ... William [Purdy] their son was accidentally killed at New Delaval Pit December 24th 1890 aged 15 years.'

William was the son of Richard and Elizabeth Purdy and is commemorated underneath his sister. William was also a Putter and as he was going into the coal face with his pony a large stone fell from the roof on to him.

> 'In loving memory of... Thomas William [Cooper] their son who was accidentally killed in Foster Pit New Delaval Decr 1st 1884 aged 14 years.'

Thomas was the son of Benjamin and Jane Cooper and is commemorated on the base of his parents' cross. Thomas was a Driver who drove the horses on the main road underground and he was killed by being crushed by tubs on the horse way.

What links all these graves is the age at which the boys died. They would not have had a large footprint, if any, in the historical records and without the information that their commemoration provides, they would be relatively unknown. However, it was not just children who suffered with accidents down the coal pits, it was men too.

> 'In affectionate remembrance of John Long the beloved husband of Sarah Long who was killed at New Delaval Colliery Feby 18th 1873 aged 36 years.'

John was a 'Hewer' and was killed by a fall of stone.

> 'In memory of … William their son and beloved husband of Ann Maughan was killed in Bebside Pit August 26th 1898 aged 55 years.'

William was the son of George and Jane Maughan and is commemorated on the family stone along with his parents siblings and wife. William was a Hewer and was killed when a fall of stone came away. The accident was reported in the *Daily Chronicle* on 27 August 1898 and the inquest into the accident reported in the *Shields Daily News* 30 August 1898 and the jury ruled an accidental death.[28] However, this is not the end to this tale; on 22 April 1899 the *Morpeth Herald* reported under the title 'The Operation of Compensation Act At Local Collieries', that Ann Maughan was given £224 11s 3d compensation.[29] The compensation was paid under the Workman's Compensation Act 1897 which allowed employees to sue their employer for compensation if they were injured/died at work, without the burden of proof falling to them, now all they had to do was show they were injured on the job.[30]

Also at Holy Trinity churchyard Seghill, Northumberland, is the gravestone of the Scott family who tragically lost family to accidents at the mines.

> 'In loving memory of Thomas the beloved husband of Mary Scott who was accidentally killed by a fall of coal in the Foster Pit Seaton Delaval July 6th 1870 aged 41 years. John their son was accidentally killed by the breaking of the apparatus chain at the North Pit Seaton Delaval, Sept 20th 1869 aged 16 years.'

Thomas was a Hewer, digging in the coal seams underground. His gravestone gives us all the same information that the *Newcastle Daily Chronicle* on 8 July 1870 did, with only a two-line entry which stated that Thomas Scott died from a fall of coal in Fosters Pit.

## Murder

This was something I really didn't expect to find, but the following gravestones give details of the fact that the persons buried there were murdered.

> **LINCOLN POSTBOY**
>
> WHO BLEW HIS OWN "DEATH PEAL."
>
> TWO ROGUES CONFESSED 65 ROBBERIES.
>
> From three contemporary accounts in his own collection, Mr. W. V. Morten, 29, Forest-road, W., Nottingham, sends us (says the "Nottingham Guardian") vivid extracts recalling the fate of the postboy of Lincoln, who was forced by his murderers to blow his horn, and then informed that it was his "death peal." Mr. Morten has rescued from oblivion the tombstone erected to the memory of the unfortunate youth. The following are the extracts:—
>
> "Tuesday, 2nd January, 1733, one William Wright, a youth of about 18 years, was found at Faldingworth Gate, near Market Rasen, lying in a chaise with his head almost severed from his body, and covered with the seat cloth. The two men suspected to be the murderers were described in the 'Gazette,' and a reward offered. They were taken at the end of December last, and confessed to sixty-five robberies and another murder."
>
> "On Tuesday, 20th February, were brought to Lincoln Gaol the two rogues who murdered the young man in the chaise. They are named Hallam, being brothers; on entering Lincoln they were treated with the utmost ignominy and reproach; one of them was for murdering all they attacked, and when taken upbraided the other with hindering him from doing it, as the chief cause of their being apprehended. They forced the postboy on the road to blow his horn, then told him it was his death-peal, and immediately cut his throat, and that of his horse. The postboys greeted them as they passed through Lincoln, in the same manner, sounding their horns, on which one of the malefactors wept."
>
> "Friday, 23rd March, were executed at Lincoln, Isaac and Thomas Hallam, for the murder of William Wright, of Market Rasen, and of Thomas Gardiner, the Lincoln postboy, on 3rd January last (1732). Whilst in gaol they confessed they had committed upwards of 50 robberies, and after condemnation, attempted to break out of prison by sawing off their fetters with a case knife, notched like a saw, and digging through the wall with a large nail, but being discovered they then, and not before then, began to think seriously of their approaching end. In passing to execution, near the place where they murdered the postboy, Isaac fell into violent agonies and perturbation of mind; at the tree, having no clergyman to assist him, he beckoned to one who was there as a spectator, who readily complied with his request, and prayed with him fervently, after which being turned off; and his brother Thomas, seeing him hanging in the air struggling for life, shrieked out dreadfully at the shocking sight, and was then led to execution nigh the place where they had murdered Mr. Wright. He as well as his brother, acknowledged the justice of his sentence, and calling upon God, was turned off."
>
> Mr. Morten observing that these accounts in the phraseology of the time vividly bring to mind the shocking scenes which were witnessed by our forefathers, on all too frequent occasions. Thomas Gardiner was only 19 at the time he was so barbarously murdered in the execution of his duty.

*Newspaper article detailing the murder of Thomas Gardiner,* Lincolnshire Chronicle *22nd May 1913, British Newspaper Archive.*

In All Saints' churchyard Nettleham, Lincolnshire, is the badly worn grave of Thomas Gardiner.

*'Thos Gardiner Post Boy of Lincoln Barbarously murdered by Isaac Tho Hallam Jan 3 1732 aged 19.'*

This gravestone has been part of the local legends in Nettleham for many years with the local newspapers running various articles on the stone. The earliest of these that I have come across so far has been that of *The Lincolnshire Chronicle* 22 May 1913. It describes that fateful night in 1732 when Thomas Gardiner was murdered by Isaac and Thomas Hallam. Both men were arrested for the murder and subsequently hanged.[31]

In St Benedict churchyard Scrivelsby, Lincolnshire, is the gravestone of Richard Tasker.

*'Sacred to the memory of Richard Tasker Gamekeeper aged 20 years who was cruelly murdered Feby 1850.'*

We know from his stone that Richard was a gamekeeper, and from the newspapers we can find out what happened. The *Leeds Intelligencer* on 9 February 1850 ran a small article telling of his murder. Richard was working as a game-watcher for Rev. J. Dymoke and was killed by a gang of poachers who trespassed on the land.[32] In St Nicholas churchyard Dersingham, Norfolk, I came across the curious grave of Daniel Arthur Sell.

*'In loving remembrance of Daniel Arthur the second and beloved son of Daniel and Harriet Sell who was killed by a gun at Sandringham House November 13th 1880 in the 16th year of his age.'*

This was a tragic accident at the home of Daniel's employer. When Daniel's father, also called Daniel, died in 1915 at the age of 79, the *Lynn News and County Press* retold the story of his son's tragic accident as part of his obituary.

It transpired that while Daniel senior was working, his son Daniel and another youth went into the gun room and, on examining a rifle and showing his companion how to put a cartridge into it, the gun went off and tragically killed young Daniel.[33]

How a person died, especially in tragic, accidental or controversial circumstances, is still something we see today, we just have different ways of getting the information across i.e. through social and mass

## SANDRINGHAM.
### A SHOOTING TRAGEDY RECALLED.

A Sandringham tragedy of thirty-five years ago is recalled by the death, which occurred at Sheringham on Saturday, of Mr. Daniel Sell at the age of 79.

In 1880, while Mr. Sell was one of the keepers on the Sandringham estate, one of his sons, Daniel Arthur Sell, aged 16, was the victim of an extremely sad shooting accident. His duty was, on the occasion of a ball on the night of November 13 in the year named, to "look after the gas." Between times he and another youth went together into the gun room. Young Sell was examining a rifle and, at the request of his companion, was showing him how a cartridge was put in when the weapon went off and young Sell's brains were blown out. Queen Alexandra herself broke the terrible news to the mother of the lad, who then resided with her husband and family at Beech Plantation.

Before entering the service of King Edward as gamekeeper, the late Mr. Daniel Sell acted for a number of years in a similar capacity to Sir Somerville (then Mr.) Gurney, and on leaving the employment of Mr. Gurney he acted as gamekeeper for some years to the late Lord James of Hereford (then Sir Henry James). When Mr. Sell was taken ill on one occasion Sir Henry sent him to the Hunstanton Convalescent Home, where he stayed for three weeks. After leaving Sir Henry James' service, some 15 years ago, Mr. Sell went to live in retirement at "Penerdene," Sheringham.

Mr. Sell, who married a Miss Allflatt, of Middleton, a sister of Mr. C. Allflatt, of Lynn, had been a widower for some years. He leaves four daughters and a son. The son is Mr. H. C. Sell, formerly steward of the Cackelose Conservative Club, Downham, and now steward of the Conservative Club at Lynn.

*Daniel Sell senior obituary, Lynn and County Press 15th May 1915, British Newspaper Archive.*

media. This was not the case for our ancestors and sometimes the only way to get an opinion heard about a tragic death was to memorialise it on the gravestone, to set it in stone for future generations to see.

*Chapter 6*

# A SENSE OF PLACE AND BELONGING

People want to feel like they belong, it is human nature. Whether that is a team, sport, group, or a place. But how do we know where our ancestors found a sense of belonging, or the place from which they originally came? In some cases the census records can help us as there is space for birthplace. However, as with any document that is dictated and then transcribed, there can be discrepancies by the enumerators on the original document and then transcription errors. This then is where the gravestones can help. In this chapter I am exploring the way our ancestors have identified themselves with a place and their sense of belonging. To do this I have taken a case study of the five medieval parish churches in the city of Leicester (as this is where many of my ancestors originated and where I have spent a lot of my time), but the results and processes I have used can be translated to other cities, towns, villages and churchyards. The churchyards that I have looked at are the five main parishes in the city: St Martin's Church (now cathedral), St Mary De Castro Church, St Margaret's Church, All Saints' Church, and St Nicholas Church. Both St Martin's and St Mary De Castro Church are in the centre of the city and are very wealthy parishes, evidenced by the large number of ornate gravestones and the vast array of large and exquisite internal monuments. St Nicholas' Church even though it is in the city centre was one of the poorest parishes, which again is shown by the fewest gravestones and the least number of internal monuments. St Margaret's Church is situated on the outskirts of the city limits but has the largest parish and with that the largest combination of the social classes. All Saints' Church is also on the city limits at the medieval gate entrance, which is why the road it sits on is called Churchgate. This again is a parish with all types of social class but is a lot smaller than its neighbour St Margaret's.

Today, as with most cities, Leicester is home to many people who have come from all over the country and the world. Some have come to work, others to see or be close to family and friends. With the roads, railway networks, sea transport and air travel we have today it is easy for people to move around the country and the world to live and work. To many people the place they call home is where they grew up, or from where they originated, and many want to be brought back there when they die. The place from which someone originates can have a physical effect on him or her too. Where you come from, or have lived for a period of time, can shape the accent you have and the language you speak. However, belonging to a place can have different meanings.

During the seventeenth, eighteenth and nineteenth centuries, it was very common to find a person's origin written on their gravestone or memorial. It can be a simple phase such as 'of this parish', or it might state the house they lived in, or the town or village they were from. After the world wars, having your place of origin, or last residence, on your stone virtually disappeared.[1]

I am going to look at where the people buried in the churches and churchyards came from, and what language they used to describe this; why they came to be in Leicester churchyards, and what other sense of belonging has been left on the memorials – such as where they are buried.

## Where people came from

The gravestones and memorials reveal that Leicester during the last few centuries had a very diverse population. In Keith Snell's work *Parish and Belonging,* the most common phrase that is found on the stones and memorials is 'of this parish'.[2] However, in Leicester churchyards this is not the case. The statement that appears most often is not a statement at all but is the specific place they came from or lived in. There are just under twenty mentions of the term 'of this parish' in its own context across the churches and churchyards. However, it is commonly found alongside occupations such as 'clerk of this parish', or after the name of the area or house that they lived in. This is also true of the term 'of this borough'. This is especially associated with the political occupations and is only mentioned six times in its own context. Another term that is also seen is 'of this town'. This applies to the town of Leicester as a whole and not a specific parish, and it appears six times; 'of this city' however, is not mentioned because Leicester didn't gain city status until 1919.

*Map showing where people came from across Great Britain, drawn by the author.*

The map shows the areas that people came from across Britain and the amount of people that have written that they come from each area on their memorials.

Apart from areas in the county of Leicestershire, which will be discussed later, London has the highest number of people that have stated they come from, or have an affinity to, the city on their stone. A couple of the individuals state that they come from London, with reference to a job.

> 'Here Lyeth the body of Sarah the daughter of Edward Allen late citizen and stationer of London by Sarah his wife she departed this life 18th day of September 1744 aged 8.'

*Gravestone of Sarah Allen her father a Stationer of London St Martin's churchyard Leicester.*

Sarah Allen was only 8 when she died at Leicester, yet I have found no other relatives buried in Leicester for her. As her stone states her father was a citizen of London and a stationer. In 1716 Edward Allen was an apprentice to a master stationer in the City of London.[3] Was he in Leicester on business with his daughter? Did they move back to London afterwards? We may never know; however, it is London that they wanted their daughter to be associated with through her father.

Another is inside St Martin's Church. It is the memorial to Robert Orpwood:

*'Here lyeth buried the bodie of Robert Orpwood Citizen and Goldsmith of London born in Abingdon in the county of Berks he departed this life 23rd August Anno D'm 1609. Hee did marry with Elizabeth Heyricke the daughter of Robert Heyricke of this parish and one of the Alderman of this Incorporation.'*

The stone of Robert Orpwood gives us so much information regarding his life and his sense of belonging. We know that he came to Leicester most likely for work and married into the Heyrick family, which was an upper-class and prominent family in the town, which is why he is buried in St Martin's in Leicester. We know that he was born in Abingdon and that he made it in London by being a Citizen and a Goldsmith of that city. The gravestone informs us of all the places that he belonged and what he or his relatives wanted him to be associated with.

The other stones and memorials that mention London do so in terms of the person being a citizen of London. This is shown on the elaborate stone of Dyer Simpson.

*'In memory of Dyer Simpson late a citizen of London and eldest son of John Simpson late of this burrough.'*

The stone from All Saints' churchyard states that he 'is a citizen of London'. Unfortunately, we can get no dates from this stone at the time the picture was taken as it is submerged, damaged, and has been moved from its original setting and is now standing up around the edge of the path around the outside of the church along with many others. However, on previous visits I was able to view the date of 1761. From knowing this and his father's name, by process of elimination I was able to find his apprentice record which states that on 27 November 1750 he was apprenticed to John Hopley of the Blacksmiths Company, it also tells us that he is the son of John Simpson of Leicester.[4]

Two of the other dedications go even further to affirm their identity and belonging with London and tell us where in London they are from. The memorial of John Johnson on the wall of St Martin's Church states that he was from the 'parish of Mary-le-Bone London'. The details of this stone are discussed in the Will and Legacy section of Chapter 2.

The memorial to John Harrison Esquire on the wall of All Saints' Church gives the actual street on which he lived. It states 'John Harrison

*Gravestone of Dyer Simpson All Saint's churchyard Leicester.*

Esq of Berkeley Street London'. However, it also states that he was born at Stocking Farm near Leicester. He was also brought back to Leicester for burial. It is possible that he wanted to be associated with London to show that he had made something of himself in life.

It is not surprising to find memorials and stones that state people come from London. Leicester is in the heart of the country and its rivers provided Leicestershire with a natural main highway of communication.

*Wall memorial of John Harrison All Saint's church Leicester.*

The waterways around Leicester were made navigable through the eighteenth century and the construction and improvement of the communications to London started in 1793 and was completed in 1814.[5] This was primarily for the carriage of heavy goods. This allowed merchants to transport their goods to the centre of the country and back again. Traditionally, people would travel about by horse-drawn carriages, but throughout the nineteenth century railway construction changed this. The Leicester to Swannington Railway was constructed in 1832 and was the first railway in the Midlands to be specifically constructed for the use of steam locomotives.[6] The Midland Counties Railway opened in 1840 and this was a train route to Derby, Nottingham, Leicester, Rugby and London, which closed the stagecoach services along the trunk roads.[7] With the places that are mentioned on the stones it shows that people were using these transport networks to get around, however, the vast majority of places that are mentioned on the stones are from in and around Leicestershire.

## Leicester and the County

There are approximately seventy stones and memorials that state that people are from Leicester or from areas in the county. Some of the stones mention the village that they are from, others state that they are from specific areas in the town of Leicester. Many of the areas of the town mentioned on the stones would have been independent of the town itself and would have been on the outskirts. Today these places are still there but they have been taken over by the growth of the city. The two tables below show which villages are mentioned and how many people come from those areas, and the different areas of Leicester that people came from.

Villages in Leicestershire that people were from and how many:

| Villages in Leicestershire | Number of people | Villages in Leicestershire | Number of people |
|---|---|---|---|
| Peckleton | 1 | Hinckley | 1 |
| Uppingham | 1 | Syston | 1 |
| West Cottage | 1 | Thrussington | 1 |
| Kibworth Harcourt | 1 | Stamford | 1 |
| Evington | 1 | Scraptoft | 1 |
| Minsterly Salop | 1 | Quorndon | 1 |
| Kirby Frifth | 1 | Melton Mowbray | 1 |
| Stock Golding | 1 | Tugby | 1 |
| Thurlangton | 1 | Carlton | 1 |
| Ashby-de-la-Zouch | 1 | Loseby | 1 |
| Great Easton | 1 | Loddington | 1 |
| Sutton Elms | 1 | Worthington | 1 |
| Willoby Waterleys | 1 | Stockerston | 1 |

| Areas of Leicester | Number of people |
| --- | --- |
| Leicester Forest | 1 |
| Stocking Farm | 1 |
| West Bridge | 1 |
| The Mitre and Keys | 1 |
| Terrace Lodge | 3 |
| New Parks | 1 |
| Danetts Hall | 4 |
| Westcotes | 9 |
| Castle view, Castle house | 3 |
| Neworks (Newark and New works) | 4 |
| Bishops Fee | 1 |

*The areas of Leicester people came from.*

The number of villages mentioned show that the five parishes of Leicester are 'open parishes'. The property within those areas was not in the hands of one, or a few, large proprietors, but in the hands of many – and this meant it was hard to control who came into and out of the parishes, but it allowed the population of the town to grow rapidly.[8] Migration to other areas and villages was something that affected every county in the country. The usual type of migration was that of servants, apprentices and would-be spouses moving to the areas for work or to live with their husband or wife (though it was usually the woman who moved to her husband's settlement). Other times it was people who wanted to make a better life for themselves and so would usually travel limited distances to a neighbouring town or village.[9] With its hosiery trade and the rise in boot and shoe manufacturing, Leicester had a lot to offer people from its neighbouring villages. Migration was also an integral part of life for the poor, moving when they had to, to find work or when they could no longer be sustainable in a certain area.[10] It is also possible that those who were buried inside the churches wanted to make sure that people know where they had come from because they'd had a prosperous life and so had the right to be buried inside a church in the town of Leicester.

The places that are mentioned that are within the town of Leicester vary. There are a few memorials that name the place in which they lived.

*'In affectionate remembrance of Joseph Briggs late of the Mitre and Keys in this town who departed this life December 1833 44th year.'*

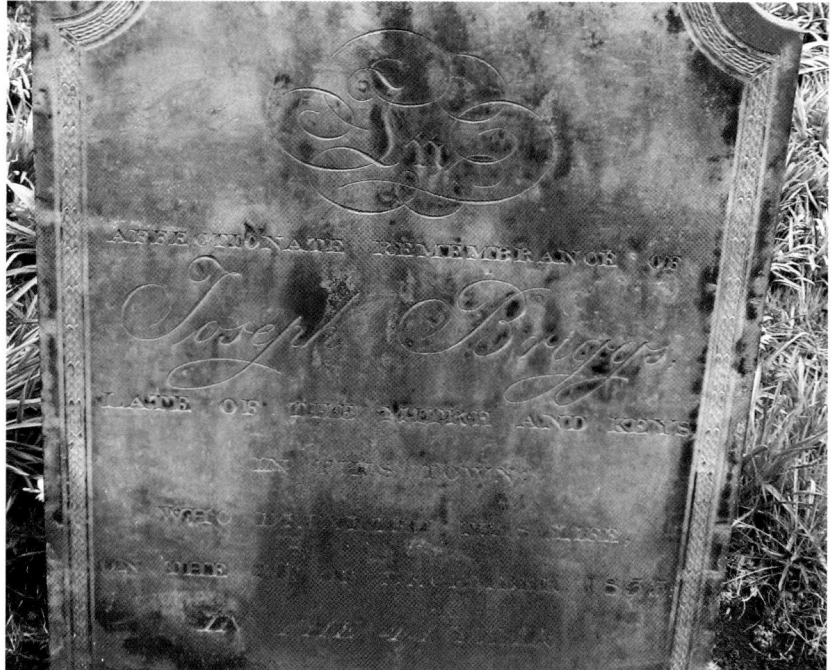
*Gravestone of Joseph Briggs St Mary De Castro churchyard Leicester.*

The Mitre and Keys was an inn on Applegate Street at the junction with West Bridge.[11] In 1826, before Joseph Briggs took over as landlord, the inn was sold and was advertised in the *Leicester Chronicle* on 11 March, detailing that it had stabling for 100 horses, houses for two gigs, a large yard and garden, and capital store rooms.[12] Joseph Briggs wanted the significance of his occupation to be remembered.

There are two other places mentioned on memorials from inside the church of St Mary De Castro. These are both areas in the town and places of residence: Danetts Hall and Westcotes. These were two large estates situated on the west side of Leicester. These are very prestigious areas and people who lived there were of very high status. Unfortunately, neither of the manors or estates now survive. The manor of Westcotes and its estate was demolished in 1885, and when the last resident of Danetts Hall died in 1861, the hall was sold for a housing development.[13]

The manor of Westcotes, which was rebuilt about 1730,[14] was situated in the area off Hinckley Road, as it is known today. There are still references to the manor as it is the name of the library on Narborough Road and the medical centre on Fosse Road North. The manor was the family home to the Ruding family, and there are nine floor slabs in the church of St Mary de Castro, each of the family members who lived at the manor have it

*Three of the nine surviving floor slabs of the Ruding family, St Mary De Castro church Leicester.*

A Sense of Place and Belonging • 111

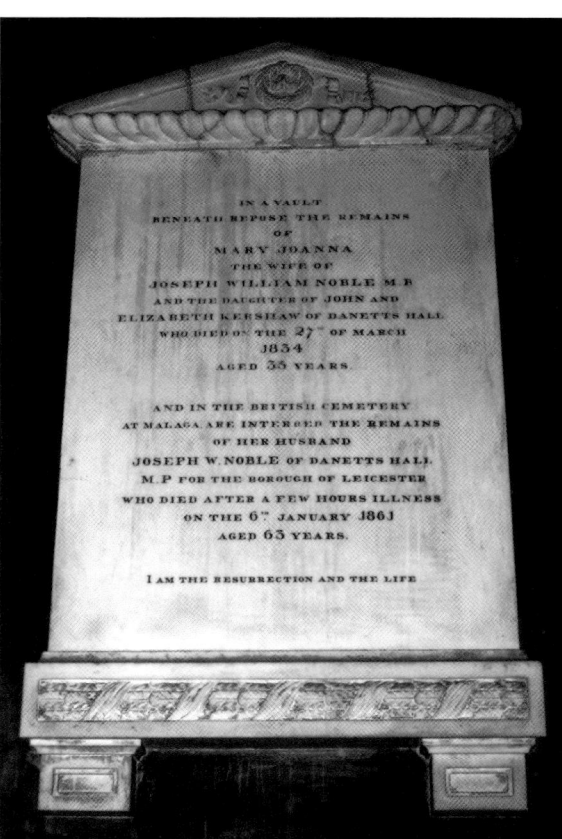

*Wall memorials showing Danetts Hall, St Mary De Castro church Leicester.*

IN A VAULT
BENEATH REPOSE THE REMAINS
OF
MARY JOANNA
THE WIFE OF
JOSEPH WILLIAM NOBLE M.D.
AND THE DAUGHTER OF JOHN AND
ELIZABETH KERSHAW OF DANETTS HALL
WHO DIED ON THE 27TH OF MARCH
1854
AGED 35 YEARS.

AND IN THE BRITISH CEMETERY
AT MALAGA ARE INTERRED THE REMAINS
OF HER HUSBAND
JOSEPH W. NOBLE OF DANETTS HALL
M.P FOR THE BOROUGH OF LEICESTER
WHO DIED AFTER A FEW HOURS ILLNESS
ON THE 6TH JANUARY 1861
AGED 63 YEARS.

I AM THE RESURRECTION AND THE LIFE

UNDERNEATH ARE DEPOSITED
THE REMAINS OF EDWARD ALEXANDER M.D.
OF DANETT'S HALL NEAR LEICESTER;
WHO DIED UNIVERSALLY LAMENTED NOVR 27TH 1822.

ALSO OF ELLEN, HIS WIFE
WHO TO THE INEXPRESSIBLE GRIEF OF HER
FAMILY AND FRIENDS,
DEPARTED THIS LIFE DECR 23RD 1825.

mentioned on their stones. With these memorials being floor slabs, not all are in good condition due to wear from continual footfall and furniture. Three of the nine that are readable are pictured.

> *'In memory of Walter Ruding Esq of Westcotes twenty-three years proprietor and thirty-one inhabitant of that place he died March 16 1818 aged 72.'*

Walter Ruding was the last male to live at Westcotes; after surviving the Napoleonic Wars his son, Captain Walter Ruding, did not want to take on the family estate, and it was sold.[15]

Unlike the manor of Westcotes, Danetts Hall was owned by several people, and each have written on their stones that they were of that place.

The manor was situated off King Richard's Road, west of the town centre, and there are no references today to the manor at all in that area. However, there are roads that are named after the people who lived in Danetts Hall. The land that the hall is built on was owned by the Danetts family from the early fifteenth century, which is where the hall got its name. It then had various owners until we come to the ones for which we have evidence:

> *'Underneath are deposited the remains of Edward Alexander M.D. of Danett's Hall* [sic] *near Leicester who died universally lamented Nov 27 1822.'*

Edward Alexander's burial record states that he was a doctor and living at Danetts Hall when he died in 1822.[16]

Danetts house was then bought by the Noble family and we have evidence for one of the last occupiers of Danetts Hall before it was sold and demolished.

> *'…Joseph W Noble of Danetts Hall M.P. for the Borough of Leicester who died after a few hours illness on the 6th January 1861 aged 63 years.'*

Due to the year in which Joseph Noble died we can delve a bit deeper with the information provided by the grave. From the 1841 and 1851 census we can see that Joseph Noble and family were living in Danetts Hall and that he had a cook and a footman. It also gives us an insight into the fact that he was an MP, and in 1851 he was a magistrate.[17] These memorials are the lasting legacy for Danetts Hall and without these we and future generations may not have known anything about this manor and estate at all.

Most of the other places named in the stones are areas of the town which are still called the same or a similar name in the city today. One that may not be recognisable however, is that of Bishops Fee. This is an area that is in the parish of St Margaret's, but it lay outside the borough boundaries. It was originally a manor owned by the Bishop of Lincoln. The Bishop's Palace was supposed to have stood on or near this site in the Saxon period as early as the seventh century.[18] There have been many disputes between the borough and Bishops Fee over the authority of the area since the twelfth century. However, it finally came under the town boundary in 1835 when the town secured the whole of the eastern suburb.[19]

The stone of John Abbott is situated in St Margaret's churchyard. He died in 1833 just before the town gained control of Bishops Fee, and he must have felt strongly that he belonged to the independent area of the parish of St Margaret's rather than state he was from the parish itself. This is the only mention of Bishops Fee from the churchyard and the church of St Margaret's.

*Gravestone of John Abbott of Bishops Fee, St Margaret's churchyard Leicester.*

The other areas mentioned on the memorials are places that still exist today. The Newarks, Stocking Farm, West Bridge, and New Parks are areas where people still live and work and still refer to them if asked where they live. Stocking farm was an area originally covered by Leicester Forest and the name means 'clearing the wood'. This area is joined to the town of Leicester via Woodgate, where firewood would be brought from the forest.[20] Today, the same as New Parks, these are areas that have had a lot of council houses built on them and are purely residential.

Castle View and Castle House, however, are rather special. Castle View is the area that is situated within the remains of eleventh-century castle walls. It consisted of a few houses and a pub, the Castle Inn; Castle House is situated on Castle Street in Leicester and this whole area around the castle is part of Leicester conservation area. This would have been a very upper-class place to live. It is the Brown family, specifically Joseph Brown, who is associated with these places in St Mary De Castro Church.

> *'In memory of Joseph Brown of the Castle View eldest surviving son of Jno and Ruth Brown ob 11 ap 1811 aet 40.'*

As you can see in the photos, the fact that Joseph Brown lived at Castle View and Castle House is memorialised on his children's wall tablets. The family wanted to be associated with that area, and the area to which their father belonged.

## Where they are buried and where they died

For someone to have a specific place inscribed on their stone or memorial, it must have meant something to them, or they particularly wanted people to know about it. The reasons are less clear when a place is included on the memorial where they are buried, but it is a place other than where the stone or memorial has been erected. There are many instances of these types of memorials dotted about in all five of the churches and churchyards.

Why did they do this? Sometimes it is purely because that is where they died, sometimes there are different reasons. In the church of St Mary de Castro as seen in the wall memorial of Mary Joanna and her husband Joseph William Noble who lived at Danetts Hall, which we have seen earlier in the chapter, Joseph is actually buried in the British cemetery at Malaga, which is stated on his stone.

> *'…and in the British Cemetery at Malaga are interred the remains of her husband Joseph W Noble of Danetts Hall M.P. for the Borough of Leicester who died after a few hours illness on the 6th January 1861 aged 63 years.'*

*Wall memorials of the Brown family, St Mary De Castro church Leicester.*

Joseph was on holiday in Malaga, Spain, when there was an outbreak of cholera and, being a doctor, he tried to help but unfortunately succumbed to the illness himself and was buried in Spain.[21]

There are other instances where a person or persons have been commemorated on a stone but are buried in other places. A vivid example of this is from Saint Nicholas churchyard. It is the stone of Robert Whitwell who died in 1825. Although he is buried in the churchyard, the rest of his family, who are all named on the stone, are buried in Leicester cemetery. We know this because the stone tells us. The reason for this is unknown, however, the dates on the stone can give us a clue. Leicester cemetery opened in 1849 due to the overcrowding of the parish churchyards in Leicester where the dead had previously been buried. Since the records began in the early fifteenth century there had been over 83,000 registered burials in the town.[22] The next inscription after Robert Whitwell is that of his wife who died in 1856, and then his children who died in 1905 and 1908. By these dates there were hardly any burials taking place in the town's churchyards. But the Whitwell family still had a connection to the parish of St Nicholas and the burial place of their father, so their names were inscribed on the same stone because that is where they belong.

In St Margaret's churchyard there is also the stone of Isabella and Thomas Langdon. They were the daughter and son of Colwell and Ann Langdon. Isabella died in 1852, her brother Thomas, who is 'buried in Leicester Cemetery', died in 1865. He is still represented on the stone

*The Whitwell family gravestone, St Nicholas churchyard Leicester.*

of his sister by his parents to show where he belonged. It isn't just cemeteries that are mentioned on stones, but also people who are buried miles away from the stone where they are being remembered.

The churchyard of St Martin's has an example of this. It is the stone of Robert Hardy. Robert died in 1841 and his wife Millicent died in 1853; the stone states at the bottom that she is 'buried in Highgate Cemetery London'.

> 'In affectionate remembrance of Robert Hardy who died July 20th 1841 in the 69th year of his age also of Millicent Hardy relict of the above who died May 31 1853 aged 75 years Her remains rest in Highgate Cemetery London.'

It is not surprising however, to find that Millicent has moved away from her hometown after the death of her husband, as the mobility of widows was common. This usually happened when where they were living became too expensive without their husband to support them.[23] From the 1851 census we know that Millicent's son Robert had a job in London as a buyer, and it is possible that she moved with him so that he could support her. Highgate cemetery was the place where the wealthy were buried in London. It opened in 1839 and many sought to be buried there and be surrounded by the rich of London.[24] However, her true place of belonging was with her husband in St Martin's churchyard.

There is also a memorial in St Margaret's Church where the commemorated died at Leicester but were interred at Kensal Green cemetery, London. This is the memorial of Alicia, Edward and Bertie Markland.

> 'In affectionate remembrance of Alicia Markland who died at Leicester April 17 1863 and was interred in Kensal Green Cemetery London. Also John Edward Markland who died at Caen in France on the 5th day of July 1863 and Bertie Markland who died at Leicester January 10th 1864 and was interred in Kensal Green Cemetery.'

From the inscription we can see that Alicia and Bertie died in Leicester. However, as the stone tells us – and which is also confirmed by the burial records for both Alicia and Bertie – they were both buried in All Souls Cemetery Kensal Green.[25] What is unclear though is why they are buried in London. As far as I can tell there was no connection, they were both born in Leicester and lived in Leicester until they died. The only clue that we have is from the 1851 and 1861 censuses. Both Alicia and Bertie were living in Leicester, but their occupation is listed as 'Railway Debentures with 9 mortgages'.[26] This means that Alicia and Bertie were wealthy enough to have loaned the government money to invest in the railways and charged them interest. This could explain why they are buried in London, it is possible that Bertie had purchased the plot in the cemetery.

By looking around the memorials inside and outside the churchyards we can get a sense of how far our ancestors travelled when the places where they died are different cities to the one they were born into, and even countries outside the United Kingdom. There is evidence of people travelling extensively and dying across the British Empire of the time, in places such as India, West Indies, Africa and the East Indies. However, most of these have a military connection.

A person's sense of belonging, as we have seen from the memorials, can be a place that they have lived in such as a pub, or an area that they feel passionate about such as Bishops Fee. It may also be the town that they originated from is different from where they subsequently lived. However, it is sometimes possible for a person to feel that they belong to more than one place, and this is shown in the stones and memorials of the those who have died in one place and then been buried in another. They feel strongly enough about the place in which they died to have a memorial or stone put up to them, but then to be buried in the place from which they originated. This is the same with family plots, people who could no longer be buried in the same churchyard as their relatives still have a sense that that is where they belong and are remembered accordingly. But they will still have a stone or memorial to where they are buried so that people will know where they are.

# CONCLUSION

It is my hope that through this book you have been able to see the value of gravestones and the wealth of information they can hold. The graves I have looked at are but a snapshot of the information that is out there to find. Gravestones can be a fantastic starting place for a research project, or the end result of years of dedicated research to discover a long-lost relative's final resting place.

They give us a fantastic glimpse into the lives of our ancestors from the biographical details of family and occupations, to the achievements and the legacy they want to leave behind. But also, the way in which they died and where they are buried. Combining the monument's details with historical documents and newspapers can give a fuller picture into the lives of our ancestors.

Each parish churchyard is a small microcosm of the people who lived there during that time, and it shows us the changing styles and beliefs of the people who died and who lived. Every gravestone and monument has a story to tell, some have many, especially if we can look past the sombre feelings and macabre notions that can often be associated with gravestones. They can tell us as much about the living as well as the dead, because the most important thing to remember is the dead do not bury themselves.

# NOTES

**Chapter 1: Symbolism, Wording and Beliefs**
1. www.funeralguide.co.uk accessed 15.07.23.
2. K. Basford, 'A new view of Green Man sculptures', *Folklore,* 102, 2, (1991), p.237.
3. Basford, *Green Man*, p 238.
4. B. Wilsher, *Understanding Scottish graveyards* (Edinburgh 1995)
5. Basford, *The Green Man*.
6. H. Mytum, *Recording and Analysing Graveyards* (London, 2000), p.36.
7. F. Burgess, *Churchyard Memorials*, p.178.
8. H. Mytum, *Recording and Analysing Graveyards* (London, 2000), p.51.
9. S. Tarlow, 'Death and Disgust in later historic Britain', in S. Tarlow and S. West (eds) The Familiar Past?: Archaeologies of Later Historical Britain (London 1999), p.193.
10. N. Lowe, *Mastering Modern British History* (London 1998), p.165.
11. J. Walvin, A child's world: a social history of English childhood, 1800–1914 (London 1982), p.43.
12. R. Richardson, *Death Dissection and the Destitute* (London 1988), p.22.
13. E. Chadwick, 'Report on the Sanitary Condition of the Labouring Population for Great Britain' (London 1842), p.32. Accessed via the National Archives 15.6.2023.
14. T. Gray, 'Elegy written in a country churchyard' in S. Winder (ed.) *Elegy written in a count churchyard and other poems* (London 2009) pp.23-28.
15. E. Chadwick 'Report on the Sanitary Condition of the Labouring Population for Great Britain' (London 1842), p.84. Accessed via the National Archives 15.6.2023.
16. *London Evening Standard* 20 Octoer 1897 p.2 www.findmypast.co.uk retrieved 8.5.24.
17. *Times* London 6 May 1917 p.6 reference GALE | FP1801784426 www.gale.com retrieved 17.8.23.
18. *Times* London 21 August 1927 p.13 reference GALE | FP1800960222 www.gale.com retrieved 17.8.23.
19. *Weekly Dispatches* (London) 4 October 1829 p.4 www.findmypast.co.uk retrieved 07.5.24.

20. 2 & 3 Will. IV c.75: Anatomy Act 1832.
21. 25 Geo. 2c. 37: The Murder Act 1752.
22. A handwritten report that is on display on the wall, on the right side of the south porch in St Margaret's church. Transcribed by the author August 2011.
23. *'Lambeth Street Resurrection Men'* London Morning Post 21 January 1821 p.2 www.findmypast.co.uk accessed 21.1.24.
24. *Drakards Stamford News* 7 April 1826 p.4 www.findmypast.co.uk retrieved 7.5.24.
25. Richardson, *Death, Dissection*, p.76.
26. E. Chadwick, 'Report on the Sanitary Condition of the Labouring Population for Great Britain' (London 1842), p.94-94. Accessed via the National Archives 15.6.2023.
27. *Weekly Globe* London 4 January 1826 p.4 www.findmypast.co.uk retrieved 7.5.24.
28. J. Rugg, 'From Reason to Regulation: 1760–1850' in Jupp & Gittings (eds) *Death in England: An illustrated History* (Manchester 1999), p.204.
29. G. Behlmer, Grave Doubts: Victorian medicine, moral panic and signs of death. *Journal of British Studies,* 42, (2) (2003) p.218.
30. K. B. Thomas, John Snow, 1813–1858. *The Journal of the Royal College of General Practioners,* 16 (2) (1968) p.92.
31. Thomas, *John Snow* p.89.
32. As cited in Behlmer, *Victorian Medicine* p.206.

**Chapter 2: Children, Family and Ancestors**
1. M. Elliott, *Victorian Leicester* (London, 1979), p.86.
2. F. Burgess, *English Churchyard memorials*, (London 1963), p.275.
3. 4 & 5 Will 4. C. 76 Poor Law Act 1834
4. P. Keating, Into unknown England, 1866–1913: selections from the social explorers (Manchester 1976), pp.304-5
5. J. Walvin, *A Child's World: A Social History of English Childhood 1800–1914,* (London 1982), p.20.
6. J.M. Strange, *Death Grief and Poverty in Britain 1870–1914,* (Cambridge 2005) p.240.
7. J.T. Biggs, *Leicester: Sanitation versus Vaccination,* (London 1912) p.188.
8. A. Goodman and G Amelagos, Infant and Childhood Morbidity and Mortality Risks in Archaeological Populations. *World Archaeology* 21 (2) 1989 p.226
9. Elliott, *Victorian Leicester pp*.90-91.
10. Biggs, *Sanitation*, p.189.
11. Stan and Trevor Yorke, *What the Victorians got wrong*, (Berkshire 2008) p.53.
12. R.A Mckinley (ed), 'The City of Leicester: Social and administrative history since 1835', *A History of the County of Leicester: volume 4: The City of Leicester* (1958), p.251.
13. E. Chadwick, *Report on the Sanitary Conditions of the Labouring Population of Great Britain,* (London 1893).
14. McKinley, *City of Leicester* p.251.

15. Biggs, *Sanitation* p.716.
16. J .Moore, *A Report on the Sanitary condition of Leicester in 1860* (Leicester 1861).
17. L. Davidoff and C. Hall, *Family Fortunes: Men and Women of the English Middle Class 1780–1850,* (London 2002) p.xxvi.
18. W. Coster, *Family and Kinship in England 1450–1800,* (London 2001), p.65.
19. OED entry for 'relict'
20. 1901 Census Harriet Lancaster www.ancestry.co.uk retrieved 12.10.23
21. P. Aries, *Western Attitude Towards death from middle ages to the present,* (London 1994) p.63.
22. Wills and administrations after 1858 – The National Archives retrieved 26.4.24.
23. Wills and administrations after 1858 – The National Archives retrieved 26.4.24.
24. Leicestershire wills and probate records 1500–1939 1825 T Clark www.findmypast.co.uk retrieved 26.4.24.
25. Bank of England Will Extracts 1717–1845 Leicestershire 1833 Elizabeth Mason www.findmypast.co.uk retrieved 26.4.24.
26. C. Gittings, 'Eccentric or Enlightened? Unusual burial and commemoration in England, 1689–1823.' *Mortality* volume 12 (4) 2007. pp.321-346.
27. J. Flanders, *The Victorian House Domestic life from childhood to deathbed,* (London 2003) p.335.

**Chapter 3: Occupations**
1. S. Barker et al, *An Atlas of English Surnames,* (Frankfurt 2007), p.201.
2. J. Storey, *Historical sketch of some of the principal works and undertakings of the Council of the Borough of Leicester since the passing of the Municipal Corporations Reform Act … with a complete list of mayors, magistrates, aldermen, councillors, and head officials, down to the present date,* (Leicester 1985) p 1.
3. P. Bryan, *The Leicester Guildhall, A Short History,* (Leicester 2011), p.2.
4. OED 'Justice of the Peace'.
5. J. Storey, *Historical sketch* p.1
6. J. Simmons, *Leicester: The Ancient Borough to 1860,* (London 1983), p.68.
7. J. Simmons, *Leicester: The Ancient Borough to 1860,* (London 1983), p.68.
8. J.T. Biggs, *Leicester: Sanitation versus Vaccination,* (London 1912), p.53.
9. J. Lee, *Who's buried where in Leicestershire,* (Leicester 1991), p.174.
10. 5 & 6 Wm. IV., c.76 The Municipal Corporations Act 1835.
11. G.B. Finlayson, 'The Politics of the Municipal Reform 1835', *The English Historical Review* 31 (1966) pp.673-4.
12. R.A Mckinley (ed) 'The City of Leicester: Social and administrative history since 1835', *A History of the County of Leicester: volume 4: The City of Leicester* (1958) p.251
13. Lee, *Buried in Leicester* p.174.
14. Bryan, *Guildhall* p.10. The selling of the Great Mace is written in an asterisk in J. Storey, *Historical sketch* p.3 with other items that are sold.
15. J. Storey, *Historical sketch* p.2.

16. M. Wade-Matthews, *The monuments of Saint Martin's Church Leicester* (Loughborough 1994), p.17.
17. *Cambridge University Alumni 1261–1900*, www.ancestry.co.uk retrieved 15.11.23.
18. *Will and probate England and Wales National Probate Calendar (index of Wills and administration 1858–1995*, p.94 www.ancestry.co.uk retrieved 15.11.23.
19. *Leicester Chronicle* 18 October 1823 p.1 www.findmypast.co.uk retrieved 17.11.23
20. *Medical Register for 1913* p.813 Jacobsen www.findmypast.co.uk retrieved 9.5.24.
21. *Passenger Lists leaving UK 1890–1960* www.findmypast.co.uk retrieved 9.5.24.
22. CLRO QS32/3 buildings
23. R.A. Mckinley, 'The ancient borough: All Saints", *A History of the County of Leicester: volume 4: The City of Leicester* (Leicester 1958), p.338.
24. J. Howard, *The state of the Prisons in England and Wales* (London 1777)
25. B. Stout, *Applied Criminology* (London 2008), p.69.
26. 43 Eliz I cap. 2 The Poor Relief Act 1601.
27. Stout, *Criminology*, p.69.
28. LRO QS32/3 buildings.
29. K. Thompson, 'The Building of the Leicester union workhouse 1836–1839' in D. Williams (ed) *The Adaptation of change. Essays upon the history of the 19th century Leicester and Leicestershire,* (Leicester 1980), p.59.
30. M. Elliott, *Victorian Leicester*, (London 1979), p.22.
31. Pigot's Directory of Leicestershire 1822, p.213
32. C. Ellis, *History of Leicester 55BC-AD1976*, (Leicester, 1976), p.94.
33. Mckinley, *Social and Administration since 1835*, p.251.
34. MasterMariners.www.rmg.co.uk/Collections/research-guides retrieved 06.01.24.
35. US Newspaper Extractions from Northeast 1704–1930 Massachusetts USA Call number 485704. www.ancestry.co.uk retrieved 02.11.23.

**Chapter 4: Military Gravestones**
1. *UK, Royal Hospital Chelsea: Regimental Registers of Pensioners 1713–1882* Jno Chelton www.ancestry.co.uk retrieved 16.4.24.
2. https://www.nam.ac.uk
3. *UK, Royal Hospital Chelsea: Regimental Registers of Pensioners 1713–1882* Henry Dawkins www.findmypast.co.uk retrieved 17.4.24.
4. *London Gazette* issue 15188 p.995-996 28 September 1799. www.thegazette.co.uk retrieved 9.5.24.
5. Lloyds List 1799–1800 www.maritimearchives.co.uk/lloyds-list retrieved 9.5.24.
6. *Leicester Journal and Midland Counties General Advertiser* Obituary 21 October 1814
7. *UK Army Registers of Soldiers Effects 1901–1929* www.ancestry.co.uk, *Anglo-Boer War Records 1899–1902* www.findmypast.co.uk retricved 07.09.23.
8. https://www.cwgc.org/who-we-are/our-story

9. *WWI British Army Service Records 1914–1920* www.findmypast.co.uk retrieved 08.09.23.
10. *UK British Army Register of Soldiers Effects 1901–1929* p.316 https://uk.forceswarrecords.com retrieved 07.09.23.
11. *Registers of Reports of Deaths: Naval Rating Blyth-Clapham.* https://www.findmypast.co.uk retrieved 13.9.23.
12. *UK, WWII, London Gazette Military Notices 1939–1945* p.3099 https://uk.forceswarrecords.com retrieved 07.09.23.
13. *Louth Standard* 1 August 1942 p.3. http://www.findmypast.co.uk retrieved 13.9.23.
14. *Daily Mail* Saturday March 2, 1946, p.3. https://go.gale.com retrieved 13.9.23.
15. *Louth Standard* 9 March 1946 p.4. http://www.findmypast.co.uk retrieved 13.9.23.
16. *Louth Standard* 14 September 1940 http://www.findmypast.co.uk retrieved 13.9.23.
17. *Lincolnshire Echo* 26 January 1998 p.6 www.findmypast.co.uk retrieved 26.3.24.
18. *Airman died in Second World War* 1939–1946 www.findmypast.co.uk retrieved 25.3.24.
19. *England and Wales National Probate Calendar Index of Wills and Administration 1858–1995* www.ancestry.co.uk retrieved 25.3.24.
20. *Louth Standard* 7 September 1946 p.4 www.findmypast.co.uk retrieved 9.5.24.
21. *Lynn Advertiser* 16 August 1918 p.5 www.findmypast.co.uk retrieved, 25.9.23.
22. *UK, RAF Officers Service Records 1918–1919* www.ancestry.co.uk retrieved 18.3.24.
23. *Airman Died in the Great War 1914–1919* www.findmypast.co.uk retrieved 08.08.23.
24. England and Wales National Probate Calendar 1918 p.69. www.ancestry.co.uk retrieved 21.09.23.
25. Casualty war details 2802427 www.cwgc.org retrieved 23.3.24.
26. https://saintronans.co.uk/alumni/IsaacPeytonSheldonHadley. Viewed 19.3.24.
27. *UK WWI Recipients of the Military Cross 1914–1920.* www.findmypast.co.uk retrieved 18.9.23.
28. Life story: Peyton Sheldon Hadley | Lives of the First World War (iwm.org.uk) viewed 23.3.24.
29. 1911 census www.ancestry.co.uk retrieved 23.3.24.
30. *UK Army Registers of Soldiers Effects 1901–1929* www.ancestry.co.uk retrieved 25.3.24.
31. *Register of reports of Deaths: Naval ratings ADM 104/130* www.findmypast.co.uk retrieved 23.3.24.
32. *Lynn Advertiser* 6 August 1943 p.6 www.findmypast.co.uk retrieved 18.9.23.
33. 1939 Register www.ancestry.co.uk retrieved 23.3.24.

34. *UK World War II Index to Allied Airmen Roll of Honour 1939–1945* www.ancestry.co.uk retrieved 25.3.24.
35. *Yorkshire Post and Leeds Intel* 17 August 1943 www.findmypast.co.uk retrieved 25.3.24.
36. *Lynn Advertiser* 4 June 1943 p.5 www.findmypast.co.uk 25.3.24.
37. 1921 Census www.findmypast.co.uk retrieved 25.3.24.
38. *England and Wales National Probate Calendar Index of Wills and Administration 1858–1995* www.ancestry.co.uk retrieved 25.3.24.
39. *The London Gazette* 21 March 1939 p.1931. *UK, WWII, London Gazette Military Notices 1939–1945* https://uk.forceswarrecords.com retrieved 25.09.223.
40. *Lynn Advertiser* 19 July 1940 p.7 www.findmypast.co.uk retrieved 25.9.23.
41. *England and Wales Marriages 1837-2005* Vol 4B p.906 www.findmypast.co.uk retrieved 27.3.24.
42. *Lynn Advertiser* 6 June 1941 www.findmypast.co.uk 28.3.24
43. *Lynn Advertiser* 26 May 1944 www.findmyast.co.uk 28.3.24.
44. *Death at Sea Records* 1891–1972 www.findmypast.co.uk 28.3.24.
45. *Huddersfield Daily Examiner* 30 August 1916 www.findmypast.co.uk retrieved 28.3.24.
46. https://www.cwgc.org. W A Jewell. Retrieved 28.3.24.
47. *British Army World War I Service Records* 1914–1920. www.ancestry.co.uk retrieved 28.3.24.
48. *Passenger List Leaving UK 1890–1960* H H Tuck www.findmypast.co.uk retrieved 28.3.24.
49. *WWI Canadian Soldiers Records* Hubert Henry Tuck https://uk.forceswarrecords.com. Retrieved 28.3.24.
50. https://www.cwgc.org. H Tuck retrieved 28.3.24.
51. 1911 Census www.ancestry.co.uk retrieved 04.4.24.
52. *UK, Soldiers Died in the Great War 1914–1919* 1917 www.ancestry.co.uk retrieved 04.4.24.

**Chapter 5: How People Died**
1. Cervellin G, Longobardi U, Lippi G. 'One holy man, one eponym, three distinct diseases. St. Anthony's fire revisited'. *Acta Biomed*. 2020 Sep 11;92(1):e2021008. doi: 10.23750/abm. v92i1.9015. PMID: 33682839; PMCID: PMC7975928.
2. Steele, John Charles. 'Numerical Analysis of the Patients Treated in Guy's Hospital for the Last Seven Years, from 1854 to 1861.' *Journal of the Statistical Society of London*, vol. 24, no. 3, 1861, pp.374–401. JSTOR, https://doi.org/10.2307/2338486. Accessed 17.0424.
3. *Western Morning News* 28 June 1928 p.5 www.findmypast.co.uk retrieved 8.5.24.
4. Britain, Merchant Seamen 1835–1857 www.findmypast.co.uk retrieved 4.11.23.
5. *Echo London* 7th March 1877 p.3 www.findmypast.co.uk retrieved 4.11.23.
6. *Brixham Western Guardian* 24 February 1910 p.2 www.findmypast.co.uk retrieved 9.5.24.
7. *Western Times* 5 March 1890 p.3 www.findmypast.co.uk retrieved 9.5.24.

8. *Deaths at Sea Records 1891–1972* J Evely p 5 www.findmypast.co.uk retrieved 12.8.23.
9. Gloucester Citizen 17th December 1906 p.6. www.findmypast.co.uk retrieved 12.8.23.
10. 1871 Vessels census Ilfracombe Pearson Adams www.ancestry,co,uk retrieved 4.2.24.
11. *The Western Daily Press* 6 July 1871 p.4. www.findmypast.co.uk retrieved 4.2.24.
12. *North Devon Journal* 6 July 1871 p.8. www.findmypast.co.uk retrieved 4.2.24.
13. *Yorkshire Post and Leeds Intel* 30 July 1887 p.8. www.findmypast.co.uk retrieved 8.2.24.
14. Leicestershire burials All Saints' church 1850 p.32 www.findmypast.co.uk retrieved 10.5.24.
15. *The Leicester Chronicle* 26 and 28 March 1891 p.7. www.findmypast.co.uk retrieved 12.8.23.
16. *Leicester Journal* 28 March 1834 p.3. www.findmypast.co.uk retrieved 17.4.24.
17. *The London Standard* Saturday November 29 1884 p.3 https://go.gale.com retrieved 05.10.23
18. 1881 Census www.ancestry.co.uk retrieved 17.4.24.
19. Death Certificate www.ancestry.co.uk retrieved 03.10.23.
20. *Leicestershire Wills and Probate Records* 1500–1939 1781 C Robins www.findmypast.co.uk retrieved 06.10.2023.
21. *Nottingham Evening Post* 6 January 1888 p.3. www.findmypast.co.uk retrieved 5.10.23.
22. 1881 Census W Corah www.findmypast.co.uk retrieved 7.2.24.
23. *Staffordshire Advertiser* 8 May 1861 p.5 and *Morning Post* 11 May 1861 p.7 www.findmypast.co.uk retrieved 8.2.24.
24. 23 & 24 Vict., Cap 151 An Act for the Regulation and Inspection of Mines 1860.
25. *Morpeth Herald* 12th May 1866 p.5. www.findmypast.co.uk retrieved 15.2.24.
26. *Newcastle Chronicle* 7 December 1872 p.5 www.findmypast.co.uk retrieved 14.2.24.
27. *Morpeth Herald* 12 December 1896 p.7 www.findmypast.co.uk retrieved 19.4.24.
28. *Shields Daily News* 30 August 1898 p.3 www.findmypast.co.uk retrieved 19.4.24.
29. *Morpeth Herald* 22 April 1899 p.2 www.findmypast.co.uk retrieved 18.4.24.
30. 60 and 61 Vict c.37 Workman's Compensation Act 1897.
31. *Lincolnshire Chronicle* 22 May 1913 p.2 www.findmypast.co.uk retrieved 19.4.24.
32. *Leeds Intelligencer* 9 February 1850 p.4 www.findmypast.co.uk retrieved 19.4.24.
33. *Lyn News and County Press* 15 May 1915 p.11 www.findmypast.co.uk retrieved 6.10.23.

## Chapter 6: Sense of Place and Belonging

1. K. D. M. Snell, 'Gravestone and Belonging and local attachment in England 1700-2000' *Past and Present* 179 (2003), pp.99–100.
2. K.D.M. Snell, 'Gravestones and Belonging' in *Parish and belonging: community, identity and welfare in England and Wales, 1700–1950* (Cambridge 2006).
3. *Britain, County Apprentices* 1710–1808 Edward Allen www.findmypast.co.uk. Retrieved 29.4.24.
4. *London Apprentice Abstracts* 1442–1850 1750 Simpson, Dyer. www.findmypast.co.uk retrieved 9.5.24.
5. J. Simmons, 'Public Transport in Leicestershire 1814-80' *Transactions of the Leicestershire Archaeological and Historical Society* (1996) p.106.
6. T. J. Chander, 'Communications and a coalfield: A Study in the Leicestershire and South Derbyshire Coalfields' *Transactions and papers (Institute of British Geographers)* 23 (1957) pp.169–170
7. Simmons, 'Public Transport' p.112.
8. S. Banks, 'Nineteenth Century Scandal or Twentieth Century Model? A New look at 'Open and Close' parishes' *Economic History Review* 41 (1988), p.52.
9. P. Clark, 'Migration in England during the late seventeenth and early eighteenth centuries' *Past and Present* 83 (1979), p.59.
10. S. Page, 'The Mobility of the Poor: a case study of Edwardian Leicester' *Journal of the British Association for Local History* 21 (1991), p.112.
11. Pigots Trade Directory 1828.
12. *Leicester Chronicle* 11 March 1826 p.3 www.findmypast.co.uk retrieved 29.4.24.
13. M. Elliott, *Victorian Leicester*, (London 1979), pp.20-21.
14. M. Wade-Matthews, *The Monuments of the church of Saint Mary De Castro Leicester* (Loughborough 1993), p.25.
15. *Leicester Evening Mail* 1 September 1939 p.6 www.findmypast.co.uk retrieved 29.4.4.
16. *Leicestershire Burials* Dec 1822 Edward Alexander www.findmypast.co.uk retrieved 29.4.24.
17. 1841 and 1851 census J W Noble www.findmypast.co.uk retrieved 29.4.24.
18. J. Thomas, *The Handbook of Leicester* (Leicester 1844), p.43
19. R. A. McKinley, The ancient borough: All Saints', *A History of the County of Leicester: volume 4: The City of Leicester* (1958) p.338.
20. M. Wade-Matthews, *The Monuments of Saint Nicholas and All Saints' church Leicester*, (Loughborough 1994), p.16.
21. M. Wade-Matthews, *The Monuments of the Church of Saint Mary De Castro Leicester* (Loughborough), 1993 p.17.
22. M. Wade-Matthews, *Grave Matters. A Walk Through Welford Road Cemetery* (Loughborough 1992), p.1.
23. Page, 'Mobility of the Poor' p.113.
24. F. Barker, *Highgate Cemetery, Victorian Valhalla*, (London 1984), pp.15–18
25. *London, Church of England Deaths and Burials 1813-2003 Kensington and Chelsea Kensal Green All Souls Cemetery 1863–1868* www.ancestry.co.uk retrieved 30.4.24.
26. 1851 and 1861 Census Bertie Markland www.ancestry.co.uk retrieved 30.4.24.

# LIST OF SOURCES

**Acts**
43 Eliz I cap. 2: Elizabethan Poor Law 1601
25 Geo. 2c. 37: The Murder Act 1752
35 Geo. III cap 5: Recruiting men for the Navy Act 1785
37 Geo. III cap 4: Recruiting men for the Army and Navy Act 1786
2 & 3 Will. IV c.75: Anatomy Act 1832
4 & 5 Will. IV, c.76: Poor Law Act 1834
5 & 6 Wm. IV c.76: The Municipal Corporation Act 1835
11 & 12 Vict. c.63: Public Health Act 1848
23 &24 Vict., Cap 151: An Act for the Regulation and Inspection of Mines 1860
60 & 61 Vict. C.37: Workman's Compensation Act 1897

**Websites**
Primary sources and search engines
www.ancestry.co.uk
www.findmypast.co.uk
www.findagrave.com
www.cwgc.org -Commonwealth War grave Commission
www.go.gale.com- Primary newspaper sources
www.uk.forceswarrecords.com – War records
www.iwm.org.uk -Imperial War Museum
www.nationalarchives.gov.uk -The National Archives UK
www.dmm.co.uk – Durham Mining Museum
www.maritinearchives.co.uk
www.thegazette.co.uk – London, Military and government notifications
www.britishnewspaperarchives.co.uk

# SELECT BIBLIOGRAPHY

Aries, P., *Western Attitude Towards death from middle ages to the present*, (London 1994)
Bailey, B., *Churchyards of England and Wales*, (London 1987)
Banks, S., 'Nineteenth Century Scandal or Twentieth Century Model? A New look at 'Open and Close' parishes' *Economic History Review 41* (1988)
Barker, F., *Highgate Cemetery, Victorian Valhalla*, (London 1984)
Barker, S. et al, *An Atlas of English Surnames*, (Frankfurt 2007)
Basford, K., *The Green Man*, (London 1978)
Basford, K., A new view of Green Man sculptures. *Folklore*, vol. 102. 2. 1991
Behlmer, G., Grave Doubts: Victorian medicine, moral panic and signs of death. *Journal of British Studies vol 42 no 2* (April 2003)
Biggs, J.T., *Leicester: Sanitation versus Vaccination*, (London 1912)
Bryan, P., The Leicester Guildhall, A Short History, (Leicester 2011)
Burgess, F., *English Churchyard memorials*, (London 1963)
Cannadine, D., 'War and Death, Grief and Mourning', in J. Whaley (ed.), *Modern Britain in Mirrors of Mortality, Studies in the Social History of Death* (1981)
Clark, P., 'Migration in England during the late seventeenth and early eighteenth centuries' *Past and Present* 83 (1979)
Coster, W., *Family and Kinship in England 1450–1800*, (London 2001)
Cox, M., (ed) *Grave Concerns. Death and Burial in England 1700–1850.* (York 1998)
Davidoff, L. and Hall, C.. *Family Fortunes: Men and Women of the English Middle Class 1780–1850*, (London 2002)
Elliott, M., *Victorian Leicester*, (London 1979)
Ellis, C., *History of Leicester 55BC-AD1976*, (Leicester, 1976)
Finlayson, G.B., 'The Politics of the Municipal Reform 1835', *The English Historical Review* 31 (1966)
Flanders, J., *The Victorian House Domestic life from childhood to deathbed*, (London 2003)
Gittings, C., 'Eccentric or Enlightened? Unusual burial and commemoration in England, 1689–1823.' *Mortality* 12 (4) 2007

Goodman A., and Amelagos A., Infant and Childhood Morbidity and Mortality Risks in Archaeological Populations, *World Archaeology* 21 (2) 1989

Gray, T., 'Elegy written in a country churchyard' in S Winder (ed.) *Elegy written in a country churchyard and other poems* (London 2009)

Husbands, C., 'Gravestones and local history: problems of interpretation' *Local Historian* 14 (1980)

Howard, J., *The state of the Prisons in England and Wales* (London 1777)

Jenkins, R.P., 'Lubberly Leicestershire?' *Leicestershire Historian* (2005)

Jenkins, R., Leicestershire, The Photographic collection. A Compilation of Leicestershire People and Leicestershire at War, (Leicester 2003)

Jupp and Gittings, (eds.) *Death in England: An illustrated History*. (Manchester 1999)

Keating, P., *Into unknown England, 1866–1913: selections from the social explorers* (Manchester 1976)

Lee, J., *Who's buried where in Leicestershire*, (Leicester 1991)

Lowe, N., *Mastering Modern British History* (London 1998)

Mckinley, R.A., (ed), *'A History of the County of Leicester: volume 4: The City of Leicester' VCH*, (1958)

Murray, S., 'Military gravestones in South East Sussex' *The Local Historian*, 32 (2000)

Mytum, H., *Recording and Analysing Graveyards*, (London two thousand)

Mytum, H., 'Popular attitudes to memory, the body and social identity: the rise of the external commemoration in Britain, Ireland and New England' *Post Medieval Archaeology* 40–1 (2006)

Nichols, J., *History and antiquities of the town and county of Leicester* (Leicester 1809)

Page, S., 'The Mobility of the Poor: a case study of Edwardian Leicester' *Journal of the British Association for Local History* 21 (1991)

Richardson, R., *Death Dissection and the Destitute*, (London 1988)

Simmons, J., 'Public Transport in Leicestershire 1814-80' *Transactions of the Leicestershire Archaeological and Historical Society* (1996)

Simmons, J., *Leicester: The Ancient Borough to 1860,* (London 1983)

Snell, K.D.M., 'Gravestone and Belonging and local attachment in England 1700-2000' *Past and Present* 179 (2003)

Snell, K.D.M., *Parish and belonging: community, identity and welfare in England and Wales, 1700–1950* (Cambridge 2006)

Steppler, G.A., Britons to Arms! *The Story of the British Volunteer Soldier and the Volunteer Tradition in Leicestershire and Rutland*, (Stroud 1992)

Stewart, D.J., 'Gravestones and Monuments in the Maritime Culture' *International Journal of Nautical Archaeology*, 36 1 (2007),

Stout, B., *Applied Criminology,* (London 2008)

Strange, J.M., *Death Grief and Poverty in Britain 1870–1914*, (Cambridge 2005)

Storey, J., *Historical sketch of some of the principal works and undertakings of the Council of the Borough of Leicester since the passing of the Municipal Corporations Reform Act ... with a complete list of mayors, magistrates, aldermen, councillors, and head officials, down to the present date,* (Leicester 1985)

Tarlow, S., 'Death and Disgust in later historic Britain', in S Tarlow and S West (eds.) *The familiar past?: archaeologies of later historical Britain*, (London 1999)

Thomas, J., *The Handbook of Leicester* (Leicester 1844)

Thomas, K.B., John Snow 1813–1858. *The Journal of the Royal College of General Practitioners,* 16 (2) (1968)

Wade-Matthews, M., *Grave Matters. A Walk Through Welford Road Cemetery* (Loughborough 1992)

Wade-Matthews, M., *The Monuments of the church of Saint Mary De Castro Leicester* (Loughborough 1993)

Wade-Matthews, M., *The Monuments of Saint Nicholas and All Saints' church Leicester*, (Loughborough 1994)

Wade-Matthews, M., *The Monuments of Saint Margaret's Church Leicester*, (Loughborough 1994)

Wade-Matthews, M., *The Monuments of Saint Martin's Church Leicester*, (Loughborough 1994)

Wager, A.J., 'Three Centuries of death: a study of attitudes reflected in gravestones in Shenstone Staffordshire Churchyard' *Transactions of the Staffordshire Archaeological and Historical Society* 19 (1977)

Walvin, J., *A child's world: a social history of English childhood, 1800–1914,* (London 1982)

Williams, D., (ed) *The Adaptation of change. Essays upon the history of the 19th century Leicester and Leicestershire,* (Leicester 1980)

Wilsher, B., *Understanding Scottish graveyards.* (Edinburgh 1995)

# INDEX

Accidental death, 69, 82, 88–9, 96
Accidentally killed, 92–3, 95–6
Alderman, 37, 104
Anatomy Act 1832, 14–15
Army, 57, 59–62, 64–6, 76
Auxiliary Territorial Service (ATS), 62, 65–7

Battle of Albuera, *see* Napoleonic war
Belonging, 100–101, 104, 117–18
Body Snatchers, 14–16
Book, 8–9, 18
Bones, 2, 4, 12, 35
Bridewells, 45
Bristol, 21
British Cemetery, 75, 76, 115
British Empire, 55, 118
Buried alive, 13, 14
Burn, 14, 61, 64, 82, 89–90, 95
Burke and Hare, 15

Canal, 87
Cherubs, 7–8
Childbirth, 31–2, 82
  Pregnancies, 32
  Stillborn, 33
Children's burial, 19–21
Chloroform, 17
Cholera, 4, 12–13, 18, 25, 33, 115
Citizen, 102–104
Coal Mining, 48–9, 94
  Accidents, 94–7
Colliery, 49, 94–6
Coffin, 4, 13–14, 16, 22
Coffin collars, 16
Commonwealth War Graves Commission (CWGC), 61–74

Consumption, *see* Tuberculosis
Corporation, 37, 39–41
Corpse, 10–11, 13, 15, 18
Coroner, 42, 44, 66, 69–70, 73, 82, 84, 88–9, 95
County Gaol, 41, 44–5

Devon, 9, 31, 47–8, 56, 61, 70, 75, 83–4, 87
Dissection, 14–16
Doctor, 13–14, 17–18, 41–4, 53, 66, 112, 115
Drowned, 75, 84–8

Epidemics, 4, 12, 18, 24–5
Edward Jenner, 24
Edwin Chadwick Sanitation Report 1942, 13, 18, 25
Erysipelas, 80

Falls or falling objects, 90–4, 96
Family, 26–8
Fire, 82, 89–90, 95
Frame smith, 41, 46
France, 13, 70, 74–7, 117
Funeral, 13–14, 16, 18, 22, 35, 67–8, 74, 90–1, 93

Gamekeeper, 41, 98
Gig, 88–9, 109
Good death, 79
Green Man, 8
Greyfriars Kirkyard Scotland, 16
Gunshot, 73, 82

Hastings, 8
Heaven, 7, 74
High Sherriff/Bailiff, 37, 39

Home Guard, 62
Hosier/hosiery, 41, 46–7, 108
Hourglass, 3–4, 8
House of Correction, 41, 44–5
Housekeeper, 30, 41, 43, 51–3

Illness, 4, 18, 78–80, 82, 112–13, 115
Images, 2–10

John Moore Sanitary Conditions Report 1860, 25
John Snow, 17–18
Justice of the Peace (JP), 37–8, 43

Keeper of County Gaol, 41, 44

Language, 10–18
Legacy *see* Will
Leicester
  Bishops Fee, 108, 113, 118
  Castle View/house, 108, 114
  Danetts Hall, 108–109, 111–12, 114
  Westcotes, 108–109, 112
Leicestershire, 46, 107–14
Leicester Cemetery, 115
Liverpool, 22–3, 76
London, 14, 18, 21, 87, 89, 102–107, 118
  All Saints Cemetery, Kensal Green, 117
  Guys Hospital, 32–3, 82
  Highgate Cemetery, 117
  St Thomas' Hospital, 15
Lost at Sea, 59, 75, 84, 86
Lundy Island, 86–7

Macebearer, 37, 39–41
Manchester, 22–3
Master Mariner, 41, 47–8, 75, 84
Mayor, 37, 41, 47
Midwife, 41, 51
Migration, 108
Militia, 56–7, 61
Military Cross, 71
Mortality, 2–4, 7–9, 11–12, 18, 21, 23
  Rate, 12, 21, 24–5
  Infant mortality, 21–6, 31
Mort safes, 16

Municipal Corporation Act 1835, 40–1
Murder, 14, 97–8
Murder Act 1752, 14

Occupations,
  General, 41–9
  Political, 37–41
  Religious, 50
  Women's, 51–3
Origin, 47, 101

Parish, 9–10, 15, 19–20, 25, 34, 37, 39, 45–6, 50, 90, 104, 113
  Churchyard, 54, 62, 115
  Church, 35, 54, 100
  'Of this parish', 52, 80, 88, 101, 104
  Open parish, 108
Pauper grave, 22
Physician, 13, 43–4
Poachers, 98
Poisoning, 82
Prayer book, 9
Premature burial, 14
Principal Probate Registry, 33
Probate, 14, 30, 33, 43, 68, 70, 73, 90–1
Poor Law 1601, 45
  Act 1834, 22, 46
Public Health Act 1848, 25

Red Cross, 61
Recorder, 37–8
Recruiting Act 1795 and 1796, 59
Regulation and Inspection of Mines Act 1860, 94
Relict, 29, 59, 117
Remembrance, 2, 4, 7, 11, 16, 77
Resurrection, 7
Resurrection men, 14–15
Royal Air Force (RAF), 62, 67, 69–70, 72
Royal Navy, 56, 58–9, 62, 72

Sanitation, 12–13, 18, 24–5
Servant, 33, 41, 43, 51–2, 108
Skull, 2–4, 8, 20, 86
Smallpox, 4, 12, 18, 24–5, 80

Soul, 4, 7, 10, 12, 18
Spinster, 14, 29–30, 33, 35
Supervisor/Officer of Excise, 37–9
Surgeon, 14–15, 20, 25, 41–2, 44, 91
Symbolism, 1–29

Thomas Gray, 12
Torch, 8
Town Clerk, 37, 39
Tuberculosis, 12, 79–80
Typhoid, 61, 64

Unexplained death, 82
Urn, 4, 7, 10, 20, 59

Vaccination, 18, 24

Watching the dead/body, 12–13
War, 55–77
  Boer War, 57
  First World War, 61, 63, 71, 74–6
  Peninsular War, 60
  Napoleonic War, 60, 112
  Second World War, 61, 67, 72
Widow, 29, 33, 44, 52, 73, 86, 90, 117
Wills, 14, 33–5
Wings, 4 7
Women, 28–33
Workhouse, 15, 41, 45–6
Workman's Compensation Act 1897, 96

Dear Reader,

We hope you have enjoyed this book, but why not share your views on social media? You can also follow our pages to see more about our other products: facebook.com/penandswordbooks or follow us on X @penswordbooks

You can also view our products at www.pen-and-sword.co.uk (UK and ROW) or www.penandswordbooks.com (North America).

To keep up to date with our latest releases and online catalogues, please sign up to our newsletter at: www.pen-and-sword.co.uk/newsletter

If you would like a printed catalogue with our latest books, then please email: enquiries@pen-and-sword.co.uk or telephone: 01226 734555 (UK and ROW) or email: uspen-and-sword@casematepublishers.com or telephone: (610) 853-9131 (North America).

We respect your privacy and we will only use personal information to send you information about our products.

Thank you!